Special Diet Solutions

Healthy cooking
without wheat, gluten, dairy, eggs,
yeast, or refined sugar

Carol Fenster, Ph.D.

Savory Palate, Inc.
8174 South Holly, Suite 404
Littleton, CO 80122-4004

Special Diet Solutions

Healthy cooking
without wheat, gluten, dairy, eggs,
yeast, or refined sugar

Special Diet Solutions
Healthy Cooking Without Wheat, Gluten, Dairy, Eggs, Yeast, or Refined Sugar

Copyright © 1997
by Carol Fenster, Ph.D.

Library of Congress Catalog Card Number: 97-66356
ISBN 1-889374-00-8
Printed in the United States of America

Although the author and publisher have exhaustively researched many sources to ensure the accuracy and completeness of the information in this book, we assume no responsibility for errors, inaccuracies, omissions, or any inconsistency herein. No information contained herein should be construed as medical advice or as a guarantee that individuals will tolerate foods prepared from recipes in this book. Please consult your health professional for medical advice.

SUMMARY
1. Wheat-free, gluten-free, celiac, diabetes, cookbook
2. Wheat intolerance, gluten intolerance, food sensitivity, food allergy

For orders and information, contact:
Savory Palate, Inc.
8174 South Holly, Suite 404
Littleton, CO, 80122-4004
(800) 741-5418   (Order form at back of book)

CONTENTS

To Larry and Brett

ACKNOWLEDGEMENTS

Many people inspired me and helped me with this book.

Lisa Whaley, Certified Nutritionist, contributed excellent ideas—especially in the formative stages of this book. Maura Zazenski was always enthusiastic and supportive. Jean Yancey offered emotional support and encouragement. Special thanks to each of you.

A number of others tested recipes, tasted the dishes, or reviewed the manuscript at various stages. To each of you, I sincerely appreciate your help: Jane Dennison-Bauer; Peggy Supplee; Debora Howard; Peggy Phannenstiel; Nancy Carol Sanker, OTR; Lynn Samuel, L.P.N.; Mary Lou Bonner; Sandy Dempsey; Linda Hellow; Kay Douglas; Anne Munoz-Furlong; Rosanne Ainscough, R.D., C.D.E., Diabetes Treatment Center of Columbia Rose Medical Center; Gail Spiegel, M.S.,R.D.; Gail Bright, R.D.; Sara Jones; Janet Y. Rinehart, President of Celiac Sprue Association/USA; Cynthia Kupper, C.R.D., C.D.E., President and CEO of the Gluten Intolerance Group of North America; Leon Greos, M.D., Colorado Allergy & Asthma Centers, P.C.; and Kenneth Fine, M.D., Medical Director, Gastroenterology Physiology Laboratory of Baylor University Medical Center in Dallas, Texas, and Medical Researcher in Gastrointestinal Disease.

Also, to the students in my cooking classes at Wild Oats, Alfalfa's, and in college classes—as well as the many people in the audience at my guest speaking engagements around the country—thank you for your advice, your support, and your enthusiasm.

My View

I wrote this book because I want to help people eat the dishes they love, without the ingredients they can't have. We take eating for granted—until we have to give considerable thought to every morsel of food that touches our lips.

I should know. I suffered from chronic sinusitis most of my life until I learned to avoid my own particular food villains—especially wheat and certain wheat-related grains. For someone raised on a farm in Nebraska and who married into a wheat-farming family, this was unsettling to say the least!

To make matters worse, I have a passion for food. Yes, I am one of those people who lives to eat. I consider eating to be one of the great joys of life, so you can imagine how unhappy I was to learn that I had food sensitivities.

However, I've learned to manage my wheat intolerance and I eat the same dishes I once ate—but prepared without wheat and other ingredients that compromise the quality of my life. In the process, I learned that many other people must avoid conventional baking ingredients for a variety of reasons, so I've also learned to cook without those ingredients.

Today, I am an expert in helping people with special diet needs manage a healthy diet. Once they identify their own particular food villains (with the help of a health professional), I help them resume eating the foods they love—without the ingredients they can't have. There is almost always an appropriate substitute for a particular problem ingredient—the secret lies in knowing what the substitute is and how to use it. I've created this cookbook so you can cook without wheat, gluten, dairy, eggs, yeast, or refined sugar. You can also avoid corn or soy if you're careful to read ingredient labels

Yes, this usually requires preparing most dishes from scratch. But, as I remind my students in cooking classes—there are two major benefits when you cook from scratch: 1) you gain control over what you eat, and 2) you control the standards under which that food is prepared. And don't underestimate the psychological aspects—it's very rewarding to create a tasty dish that you, your family, and your guests enjoy.

Whenever you're tempted to eat foods that you know won't agree with you, remember. . . *Nothing tastes as good as feeling good feels.* Learn to rejoice in what you *can* eat, rather than focusing on what you *can't* eat.

To get the most benefit from this book, be sure to read the Glossary of Ingredients beginning on page 9 to learn more about the ingredients you'll be using. And you must read the Appendix to understand how certain ingredients are used in baking without wheat, dairy, eggs, yeast, or refined sugar. Always read through the entire recipe first to make sure you're prepared. And, most importantly, I hope you, your family, and your guests truly enjoy the dishes in this book. Bon Appetit!

INTRODUCTION

How To Use This Book

This book is a resource for people on special diets. It is meant to help you eat the dishes you want—after your health professional tells you which ingredients to avoid. Specifically, this book is designed to be used by people who *know* they must avoid certain ingredients—especially wheat, gluten, dairy, eggs, yeast, and refined sugar.

This book should not be used to "self-diagnose" yourself or others, to determine whether you have a particular condition that warrants a special diet, or to determine the particular ingredients you should avoid. Let a health professional guide you in this process.

Can This Book Help You?

If you belong to one or more of the following groups of people, then the recipes in this book are appropriate for your diet:

1) People who <u>must</u> avoid gluten in their diets. This includes persons with celiac disease (also known as celiac sprue, gluten intolerance, gluten sensitive enteropathy, and dermatitis herpetiformis). In addition, 5% of people with insulin-dependent (Type I) diabetes have celiac disease, so the recipes include nutrient values and food exchanges for managing this particular diet.

2) People who must avoid wheat and all wheat-related grains because of wheat allergies or intolerances or other special dietary considerations.

3) People with wheat allergies or intolerances who must *also* avoid dairy, eggs, yeast, and refined sugar—or have someone in the family who avoids them.

4) Vegetarians and vegans who want baked goods without dairy and egg products.

Why People Must Avoid Certain Ingredients

Celiac Disease

Celiac disease (also called celiac sprue and related forms of gluten intolerance or gluten sensitive enteropathy) is a genetically transmitted condition in which gluten (a protein in certain grains) destroys the small intestine's ability to absorb nutrients from food. Another form of the disease is dermatitis herpetiformis (DH) with symptoms of skin rashes and blisterlike spots. Approximately 1 in every 2,500-3,000 persons in the United States has celiac disease. Other parts of the world such as Great Britain, Ireland, and Northern Europe report a much higher incidence—1:300 in the general population. (Celiac Sprue Association news release, October, 1996)

Persons with celiac disease must avoid all forms of gluten, which is present in wheat and wheat-related grains such as barley, rye, spelt, oats and the lesser known grains of kamut and triticale. All recipes in this book avoid these grains by using gluten-free flours and by specifying gluten-free substitutes for other ingredients as well. The recipes are designed so that you can make them without gluten, with instructions for omitting additional problem ingredients—dairy, eggs, or refined sugar— if necessary.

Celiac disease is a lifelong condition and requires strict adherence to a gluten-free diet. This condition must be managed with the help of a gastroenterologist, who performs a series of tests before a final diagnosis can be made.

A particularly useful resource for this group is the Cooperative Gluten-Free Commercial Products Listing published by the Celiac Sprue Association. This publication lists products and ingredients that are gluten-free. Many other national associations provide beneficial information, as well. (See Associations in Appendix.)

Celiac Disease and Diabetes
According to Diabetes Forecast (August, 1996), approximately 1 in every 20 (or 5%) of people with insulin-dependent (Type I) diabetes also have celiac disease. And some celiacs have Type II diabetes. Both groups must avoid all forms of gluten—while monitoring the rest of their diets, as well.

How can celiacs with diabetes use this book? Each gluten-free recipe contains nutrient values and food exchanges for monitoring daily nutrient intake. (See Food Exchanges in Appendix.) Each recipe offers guidelines for using alternative sweeteners in place of refined sugar. Or, non-calorie sweeteners may be used where appropriate.

The combination of celiac disease and diabetes demands a very careful diet. Persons using these recipes are urged to work closely with their health professionals to assure a balanced diet. See the Appendix for associations that provide information on diabetes.

Food Allergies and Intolerances
Although there is not one official national statistic, food allergies are thought to affect anywhere from 1 to 5% of the general population. The Food Allergy Network says 1 to 2% of adults have true food allergies. Others estimate that over 50% of Americans suffer from food intolerances and sensitivities. Whether you are allergic (your reaction is usually sudden and more pronounced) or intolerant (your reaction may be delayed and more subtle), these recipes show you how to cook without the problem ingredients.

The ingredients most likely involved in allergies or intolerances include wheat, dairy, eggs, yeast, and refined sugar. Some people avoid dairy products because they are allergic to milk proteins, while others are unable to digest the milk sugar, lactose. Read labels to avoid corn and soy. (See the Appendix for Hidden Sources of Corn and Soy.)

Diagnosis of a food allergy or intolerance should be made by a board-certified allergist or a health professional who specializes in this area. There are a variety of tests and procedures used to confirm a diagnosis; not all experts agree on a single approach. There are also many associations dedicated to helping people with these conditions. See the Appendix for a list of these associations.

Peanuts—A Special Type of Food Allergy

Allergy to peanuts is one of the most prevalent—and serious—food allergies. All recipes in this book avoid the use of peanuts, peanut oil, and any other ingredient containing peanuts. However, carefully read all labels to make sure ingredients are peanut-free.

Candida and Yeast Conditions

In addition to diseases, food allergies, and food intolerances, there is also growing interest in avoiding yeast. There are several yeast-free bread recipes in this book and there are substitutions for ingredients that would ordinarily contain yeast such as vinegar and fruit juice concentrates. Unfortunately, people on yeast-free diets must also carefully control their sugar intake, as well. Completely avoiding yeast is quite difficult to do, so be sure to consult a health professional to guide you. See the Appendix for Hidden Sources of Yeast.

Vegetarians

Vegetarians do not eat meat, fish and poultry. Vegans are vegetarians who abstain from eating all animal products, including eggs, milk, cheese, and other dairy items. If this is your lifestyle, you'll be pleased to know that most recipes in this book contain dairy and egg-free versions of baked goods. In addition, non-animal substitutes are offered such as a vegetable-based gelatin instead of the animal-based gelatin (common brand is Knox).

Additives

A book on special diets isn't complete without mentioning food additives. All recipes in this book are intended to be as free of additives as possible because the recipes use mostly fresh, wholesome, unprocessed ingredients. However, you must carefully read labels to make sure the ingredients you choose are additive-free. In addition, use organic produce, if possible.

Labels

Reading labels is terribly important when shopping for special diets. Learn to recognize the various names used for certain ingredients. For example, many other words indicate the presence of wheat flour in prepared foods. These include all-purpose flour, unbleached flour, semolina, durum, and so on. Other words are used for eggs and dairy products, as well. See the Appendix for a list of hidden sources of problem ingredients.

Also, <u>continue</u> to read labels on all ingredients—even the ones you've used for a long time. Manufacturers may change the contents of an ingredient—perhaps adding a substance. They may change the manner in which it was prepared, such as dusting the item with wheat flour to prevent sticking. Or the manufacturing process may introduce cross contamination with other problem ingredients. Call the manufacturer if you have concerns. Remember to phrase your questions to food manufacturers as clearly and concisely as possible and be sure to thank them for responding to your questions.

Nutritional Content and Food Exchanges

Managing a healthy diet is important to all of us, so nutrient values are offered as an aid to managing your nutritional intake. These values are based on the United States Department of Agriculture (USDA) guidelines and are only approximate, since exact nutrient values may vary according to size of serving or particular brands of ingredients used.

Also, some of these values are rounded according to the Food and Drug Administration (FDA) guidelines. For example, if there are fewer than 5 grams of fat, the value is rounded to the nearest 1/2 gram. If more than 5 grams of fat, the value is rounded to the nearest whole number. Carbohydrates and proteins are rounded to the nearest whole number. Calories are rounded to the nearest 5 calories.

Data from the American Diabetes Association and the American Dietetic Association are used to calculate food exchanges for further assistance in managing a healthy diet. Exchange data for additional substitutions in each recipe are offered only if the exchanges are significantly altered by that substitution. Although these nutrient values and food exchanges tell you what is in each individual dish, it's wise to enlist the advice of a dietitian or nutritionist to assure your daily nutrient intake meets recommended levels. As with the nutrient data, food exchanges are only approximate and should be used as general guidelines. See Food Exchanges in the Appendix for additional information.

Why is Customizing Recipes Important?
Chances are, you've looked at cookbooks that either omit only a few of the ingredients you must avoid—or omit far more than you want to. This book is designed to help you customize dishes to exclude *only* the problem ingredients you and your family must avoid, leaving in the ingredients you don't want to give up.

I often hear people in my cooking classes talk about having to prepare multiple versions of the same dish to suit their family's individual food concerns. This is not only time consuming, but frustrating and inefficient—especially when one version can please everybody. In addition, when meal preparation becomes overwhelmingly difficult, it is tempting to stray from your recommended diet. This means that the symptoms you or your family want to avoid will most likely return.

Here is some additional information about how these recipes allow you to customize dishes when one or more of the following is a problem ingredient.

Flour
Instead of wheat and gluten flours, the recipes in this book use a combination of flours—rice, bean, potato starch, and tapioca. Why these flours? This combination is safest for the largest number of people, the flours are least likely to compete with the flavors of the dish, and combinations of these flours produce the most pleasing results.

In place of rice flour, many recipes use bean flour made from a combination of garbanzo (chickpea) and fava (broad) beans. This flour is ideal for people who want to increase their protein intake, provided they're not allergic to or intolerant of legumes. The flour does not alter the dish's flavor, but does impart a slightly sweeter taste than rice flour. For people who are allergic to rice, this flour might be a welcome alternative. See Baking With Wheat-

Free Flours in the Appendix for more information about this flour. (One caution: avoid this flour if you have a condition called glucose-6-phosphate dehydrogenase (G6PD) deficiency in which fava beans cause digestive problems.)

In place of potato starch, cornstarch can be substituted in a 1:1 ratio—provided you can eat corn. And 1 cup of tapioca flour can be replaced with 7/8 cup sweet rice flour. Refer to the Wheat-Flour Equivalents chart in the Appendix if you want to customize your own recipes.

Some cooks prefer to use gluten-free flour mixes that they've mixed themselves or purchased pre-mixed. I prefer to tailor my flour combinations to produce the unique characteristics required in different baked goods. For example, cakes have a different texture from muffins and both are quite unlike pizza crust. Therefore, it makes sense to use different flour combinations for different types of dishes so you can better control the results.

Also, this book provides time-saving mixes customized for the unique characteristics of the item you're baking, rather than using an all-purpose flour mix for everything. You'll find cake mixes designed for cakes, muffin mixes designed for muffins, and so on.

Eggs
People avoid eggs for three main reasons: 1) allergies, 2) vegan diets and 3) reducing cholesterol. Liquid egg substitutes (such as Egg-Beaters) still contain eggs, so they're not appropriate for the allergic or vegan diet but they are low in cholesterol. Some *may* also contain wheat or cornstarch. Most of the baked goods in this book can be made without eggs. Just look for the words "without eggs" after the recipe name. Of course, using eggs produces a "lighter" baked item. See the Appendix for Baking with Egg Substitutes.

Dairy
People avoid dairy products for three reasons: 1) allergies, 2) lactose intolerance or 3) vegan diets. If lactose intolerance is your concern, you may use lactose-reduced milk in place of regular milk in these recipes. (Some celiacs cannot tolerate lactose-reduced products.) If, however, you are allergic to dairy products or just want to avoid all dairy products for personal reasons, there are suggestions for using milk substitutes made from rice, soy, or nut milk. According to the Food Allergy Network newsletter (Vol. 5, #4, April-May, 1996), goat's milk or cheeses are not recommended for those with milk allergies since the proteins are believed to be similar. However, some people with lactose intolerance say they can tolerate goat products. Be sure to read the label on these milk substitutes to make sure no other offending ingredients are present. For example, some "dairy-free" items actually contain casein, a milk protein that must be avoided by milk-allergic persons.

There is also a new oat milk on the market. However, this is not a good solution for persons who must avoid gluten. There are also dairy-free yogurts and sour cream. See the Appendix for additional information on Baking With Dairy Substitutes and Hidden Sources of Dairy in prepared foods.

Yeast

People who can't eat yeast must avoid all breads made with yeast, but it's not that simple. In addition, on a very strict diet they might also avoid all fermented products including vinegar, fruit juice concentrate, and many condiments. And, they must limit sugar intake.

There is no direct substitute for yeast in breads, but there are many breads in this book that use other leavening agents such as baking powder or baking soda. This means you can eat sandwiches, pizza, hamburger buns, etc. You can even make your favorite condiments without yeast. See Hidden Sources of Yeast in the Appendix.

Refined Sugar

The recipes in this book are delicious—whether you use refined sugar (also known as white sugar) or a sugar alternative appropriate for that particular dish. See Baking With Alternative Sweeteners in the Appendix for guidelines about using alternative sweeteners in place of refined sugar. Experts disagree about the degree of refinement in some alternative sweeteners. You may use your favorite non-calorie sweetener in dishes where it is appropriate, but you will need to experiment to find the right combinations.

Corn

Corn is one of those ingredients that mysteriously appears in ingredient lists on commercial products—often as a filler, emulsifier, or as a sweetener (as in corn syrup). If you read labels carefully, you can make most recipes in this book without corn and you can even make your own corn-free baking powder. (See chapter on Baking Substitutes & Condiments.) See the Appendix for Hidden Sources of Corn.

Soy

There is considerable discussion these days about the health benefits of soy. Aside from those benefits, soy is used in this book for the beneficial properties it brings to cooking —namely, creaminess, moisture, and improved texture in baked goods. Many of the egg-free recipes in this book use soft silken tofu which is made from soy as a replacement for the binding qualities of eggs. Soy beverage can be used as a substitute for cow's milk. Some recipes use soy flour. However, many people must avoid soy for a variety of reasons. Check with your health professional about whether soy is appropriate for you. Read labels to see which products contain soy and see the Appendix for Hidden Sources of Soy.

BAKING WITHOUT CONVENTIONAL INGREDIENTS

All conventional baked goods usually contain wheat, eggs, milk, sugar, and a leavening agent, and each ingredient plays a unique role in producing tasty, pleasingly textured results. What happens when we omit these ingredients? Let's take each separately.

Baking without wheat flour produces a somewhat heavier and denser product because the missing gluten can't establish a cell structure in which the leavening agent does its job. However, using xanthan gum helps alleviate this situation to the extent that many people can't distinguish between the same cake made with and without wheat flour.

Eliminating eggs has as dramatic an impact on baking as omitting wheat flour. In fact, eliminating wheat flour and eggs are the two biggest challenges to allergy-free baking. Eggs not only bind ingredients together and provide moisture, they are also leavening agents. This is the function we miss the most in baking. Several other ingredients can bind and moisturize a recipe, but eliminating eggs produces baked goods that are decidedly heavier and denser. For example, a cake that is light and airy when made *with* eggs becomes more like pound cake when made *without* eggs—but is still delicious!

Using milk substitutes is quite easy and usually has a minimal impact on the final product. In fact, most non-dairy milks can be used interchangeably with cow's milk in baking. Each type of milk has subtle taste differences and may produce slight color variations in the finished product (for example, soy milk may darken the product during baking). Decide which type of milk you prefer and stick with it. Be sure it doesn't contain problem ingredients such as casein (a milk protein) or barley malt extract (which is wheat-related).

Baking without refined sugar is uniquely challenging because the sugar substitutes can be solids or liquids and they change the chemical balance in a recipe. Also, the various sugar alternatives produce unique taste sensations and somewhat different color hues. Finally, some sugar alternatives produce decidedly less sweetness. But all sweeteners produce delicious results.

Eliminating yeast means no yeast aroma or taste, but breads can be made quite successfully with other leavening agents such as baking powder and baking soda.

So, what does all this mean? Cooking without conventional ingredients is not harder—it's just slightly different. While there are a few more ingredients in each recipe, these ingredients are essential and require only a few more seconds of measuring. Also, certain ingredients cost somewhat more than conventional versions—a small price to pay for being able to resume eating your favorite dishes and maintaining a healthy diet.

PRINCIPLES OF COOKING WITHOUT WHEAT OR GLUTEN

Although cooking without conventional baking ingredients requires unique cooking techniques, omitting wheat and gluten present special challenges. Here are some guidelines for successful baking which have been incorporated into each recipe:

- Substitute rice, bean, potato starch, and tapioca flours for wheat flour

- Mixture of flours (2-3) works better than single flour

- Extra ingredients such as xanthan gum, soy lecithin, and gelatin as well as different preparation techniques restore texture and appearance

- More leavening helps raise the dough and more flavorings restore flavor

- Dough is softer, moister, and stickier than traditional dough so bread machines and heavy-duty electric mixers are efficient aids for handling the dough

In addition to these guidelines, I find it useful to sift the ingredients *after* measuring to remove unmilled grains or foreign particles. To measure dry ingredients, use dry measuring cups or spoons and level the top off with a straight-edged knife. Don't pack the flour into the cup or spoon. Use liquid measuring cups for liquids. And, use standardized measuring cups and spoons from a reputable manufacturer for consistent results.

TIPS FOR ALTITUDE ADJUSTMENTS

These recipes were developed at 5,000 feet altitude, but are not necessarily altitude-sensitive. If you're baking above 7,500 feet, no changes are usually required. At sea level, you *may* need to adjust recipes using these guidelines. It's best to follow the recipe the first time, then make adjustments (if necessary) the next time you make the dish.

- Increase baking powder or baking soda by 1/4 to 1/2. (If using acidic ingredients such as sour milk or buttermilk, no adjustments are needed.)
- Increase rising times for yeast breads by 30 minutes
- Increase each cup of sugar by 2-3 tablespoons
- Decrease liquid by 3-4 tablespoons per cup of liquid
- Decrease oven temperature by 25 degrees

Source: These tips come from the Colorado State University Cooperative Extension Bulletin 530A, 1985, and my personal baking experiences with wheat-free flours.

GLOSSARY OF INGREDIENTS

Read this section carefully before using this cookbook so you know what the ingredient is, what it looks like, and where to find it. No endorsement of products is intended, but certain brands are mentioned to help you find the ingredient. This information pertains to the United States only since brands and manufacturing processes vary by country.

Read labels carefully to make sure you know what you're eating. Continue to read labels since manufacturers can change the ingredients and the processes under which the ingredient is handled. And remember . . . *if in doubt about any ingredient, leave it out!*

Ascorbic Acid: Also called Vitamin C crystals or powder. Choose unbuffered version for maximum boost of leavening in baked goods. Found near supplements in natural food stores. (See **Vitamin C** in this section.)

Applesauce: Sold in supermarkets and natural food stores. Also available as baby food, but choose those (e.g., Gerber First) without extra fillers such as rice or tapioca. Organic versions are usually darker in color and will cause baked goods to be somewhat darker, also. Used as binder and sweetener.

Arrowroot: Flour made from a West Indies root. Excellent thickener for fruit sauces or other sauces that do not require high heat. Adds glossy sheen to foods, making them look like they contain more fat than they actually do. Found in natural food stores.

Baking Powder: Clabber Girl, Featherweight, and Watkins make gluten-free versions. See Index for a recipe to make your own corn-free, gluten-free version.

Brown Rice Syrup: A syrup made from brown rice. Generally off-limits to celiacs. However, Lundberg's new version says gluten-free on the label. Found in baking aisle.

Brown Sugar: Generally made from cane sugar, this is white refined sugar to which a little molasses has been added. Found in baking aisle of grocery or natural food stores.

Butter: Land O'Lakes butter is gluten-free. If cow's milk butter is unsuitable, use oleo. Or use canola oil spread (Spectrum™), vegetable shortening, or same amount of your favorite cooking oil. (See also **Canola Oil Spread, Oleo,** and **Oil** below.)

Butter Flavored Salt or Sprinkles: Durkee makes a gluten-free version and Butter Buds are gluten-free, but both may contain dairy. Found in baking section. Butter-flavored (gluten-free) extracts may be used instead.

Cane Sugar: Found in two forms: 1) white sugar which is highly refined, and 2) unbleached cane sugar which has more nutrients. Find unbleached cane sugar in the baking aisle of natural food stores. Beet sugar can also be used.

Canola Oil: One of the most heart-healthy oils, it has a very low smoking point which means it won't cause baked goods to brown too quickly. You may substitute other oils, such as safflower or corn—or your favorite oil. Found in the baking aisle.

Canola Oil Spread: Sold under the brand name Spectrum™ from Spectrum Naturals, this 100% canola oil spread looks and tastes like butter with the consistency of mayonnaise. Non-hydrogenated, it bakes quite well but does not melt or blend into sauces cooked on the stovetop. Its fat is mostly mono-unsaturated, so it is a healthy substitute for vegetable shortening, oleo, or butter—which you may use instead. Contains soy protein. Found in refrigerated section near the butter in natural food stores and some supermarkets.

Cheese: See **Parmesan Cheese** below and also see Baking with Dairy Substitutes in Appendix for more information on related dairy products.

Chocolate and Chocolate Chips: "Dairy-free" chocolate chips and bars are available in natural food stores, but may actually be processed on dairy equipment. Carob chips may be used in place of chocolate chips, but these chips may be sweetened with barley malt.

Coffee Powder: Taster's Choice makes a gluten-free instant coffee powder.

Cooking Spray: Read labels carefully to select a spray that doesn't contain problem ingredients (such as wheat flour or soy). Mazola and Watkins carry gluten-free versions. There are non-aerosol versions as well. Vegetable shortening or oil may be used to coat baking pans instead of cooking spray.

Cornstarch: Made from corn, this white powder is the same ingredient used to thicken sauces and puddings. Can be used as a flour in wheat-free cooking. Found in baking aisle of supermarkets and natural food stores. See Wheat-Free Flours in Appendix.

Dried Cane Juice: Choose organic version. Common brand is Sucanat®. See **Sucanat®**.

Dry Milk Powder: A white milk powder that adds sugar and protein in baked goods. Found in natural food stores near flours or in baking section. Do not use Carnation instant milk. Non-dairy versions available, but make sure they're casein-free if you're allergic to milk. See Baking With Dairy Substitutes in Appendix.

Eggs: Be sure to use large eggs. Egg whites may be used in place of whole eggs. Liquid egg substitutes may be used if they do not contain problem ingredients.

Egg Replacer: White powder made of various starches and a little leavening. May be used in addition to eggs in certain recipes or in place of eggs in others. Helps stabilize baked goods. Packaged in Ener-G box and found near flours in baking aisle of natural food store.

Extracts or Flavorings: Flavorings restore flavor to baked goods when certain ingredients are omitted. Look for alcohol-free brands including Frontier (the bottle is labeled alcohol-free), available in natural food stores. Another is Bickford, which can obtained by mail-order. See Mail Order Sources in Appendix.

Fruit Juice Concentrate (frozen): Found in frozen food section. Avoid if yeast-sensitive.

Garlic Powder or Garlic Salt: Gluten-free versions include Durkee and Spice Islands. You may also use fresh garlic instead.

Gelatin Powder: Available in regular version (most common brand name is Knox) or kosher, which is made from vegetable sources. Adds moisture and helps bind ingredients together. Found in baking aisle of supermarkets and natural food stores. Kosher versions are at some natural food stores and may be marked "pareve". You may also use agar, a vegetarian gelatin made from seaweed. It is sold in natural food stores.

Granulated Fruit Sweetener (brand name Fruit Source™): Peach-colored granules. Made from dehydrated fruit juices and rice syrup (which is usually off-limits for celiacs). However, according to the manufacturer, FruitSource™ brand is gluten-free. Found in baking aisle of natural food stores. See Baking With Alternative Sweeteners in Appendix for tips on using this sweetener—if it's approved for your use.

Guar Gum: Plant-derived gum used to provide structure to baked goods so leavening can do its job. Also used to give creamy texture to ice cream. Has some fiber so could be irritating to very sensitive intestines. Can be used in place of xanthan gum, but use half again as much guar gum to replace xanthan gum. Found in baking aisle or near bulk herbs of natural food stores.

Honey: Probably one of the most common substitutes for refined sugar in baking. Different varieties are available, each imparting a distinctive flavor and color to baked goods. Avoid giving honey to children under age 2 because of possible botulism. For safety, avoid unrefined honey.

Italian Herb Seasoning: A blend of spices and herbs, found in the spice section of all grocery stores and natural food stores. Durkee and Spice Islands are gluten-free.

Ketchup: May contain distilled vinegar, which may be grain-based. Del Monte, Heinz, and Muir Glen claim to be gluten-free. Avoid ketchup if you're yeast-sensitive. You can make your own using the recipe in the Baking Substitutes & Condiments chapter.

Lecithin Granules or Liquid: Made from soy, lecithin emulsifies, stabilizes and texturizes baked goods (especially bread). Granular and liquid versions found in the supplement section of natural food stores (usually in very large containers). Granular versions are sometimes packaged in small plastic bags in the refrigerated sections of natural food stores. Usually light or beige-yellow in color, the limited amount (about 1/4 teaspoon) required in recipes changes neither the flavor nor appearance but does enhance the texture. Buy only pure soy lecithin. Avoid this ingredient if soy-sensitive.

Maple Sugar: Maple syrup that has been dried into crystals. May lend a slight maple taste to baked goods. Available at natural food stores in baking aisle.

Maple Syrup: Made from maple tree sap and available at supermarkets and natural food stores. Most flavorful version for baking is Dark or Grade B (formerly grade C), which is often sold in bulk in natural food stores. Choose organic maple syrup to avoid formaldehyde.

Milk: People with cow's milk allergies or lactose-intolerance should use alternatives such as rice, soy, or nut milk (called beverages). Be sure the milk you choose is casein-free if you're allergic to milk. Also, the Food Allergy Network newsletter (Vol. 5, #4, April-May, 1996) does not recommend goat's milk if you are truly milk-allergic. However, most people who are milk-intolerant seem to do just fine with goat's milk.

Celiacs should avoid milk substitutes with brown rice syrup (may contain barley) or modified food starch, unless the starch source is known to be safe. Read labels to choose the milk appropriate for your condition. If all else fails, replace the milk with juice or water. However, the flavor and texture of the baked item may be affected slightly since many recipes depend on the protein in milk. See Baking With Dairy Substitutes in the Appendix.

Molasses: Thick and strong-tasting, molasses is made from cane sugar and often used as a sweetener in baking. Use unsulphured molasses, not blackstrap molasses. Found in natural food stores and supermarkets, usually near pancake syrups, jellies, and jams.

Oil: Choose 100% pure oil. The heart-healthiest for baking are canola, safflower, and corn oil—and they work well in baked desserts because they're less likely to burn. Olive oil is best in breads. Read labels to choose one best for you. See Cooking Oils in the Appendix.

Oleo: An alternative for those who can't use dairy products, vegetable shortening, or other oils in baking. Make sure oleo is gluten-free (and dairy-free, if necessary) and suitable for baking (soft versions have too much water for baking).

Onion Powder, Onion Salt, and Minced Onion: Sold in baking section, along with liquid onion and liquid garlic by Durkee. Spice Islands and Durkee make gluten-free onion salt; Magic Herbs and Spices makes gluten-free onion powder and salt; Lawry's and Watkins make gluten-free minced onion. You may also use freshly grated onion instead.

Parmesan Cheese: Usually made from cow's milk, but some versions are made from goat's milk or sheep's milk (which milk-allergic persons should avoid). Found in the refrigerated dairy or cheese sections of natural food stores. Soyco Foods makes two grated Parmesan cheeses. One is made of brown rice but contains casein, a milk protein. The other is made of soy, labeled 100% dairy free and casein-free, and contains texturized vegetable protein (TVP) which is soy-based. Store on pantry shelf until opened, then refrigerate.

Potato Starch: A fine, white powder made from the starch of potatoes. Adds a light, airy texture to baked goods. Found in the flours section of natural food stores. Don't use the heavy, dense potato flour—which is made from potatoes and their skins.

Prune baby food: Prune baby food is the simplest way to use prunes as a replacement for some of the fat in baked goods or as a binder. Choose brands such as Gerber First that have prunes only, without additional fillers or thickeners. Pureed prunes are also in the baking aisle of supermarkets or natural food stores. See the Appendix for suggestions on baking with prune puree as an alternative sweetener or binder. (Also see **Pureed Fruit** below.)

Pureed Fruit: Several fruits work nicely to help bind ingredients, add sweetness and moisture, and replace fat. Pureed pears impart little flavor or color. Pureed apples (applesauce or apple butter) impart a slight apple flavor, especially if the apple butter is spiced. The darker color and flavor of pureed prunes or dates make them useful only in darker, more strongly flavored dishes such as spice cakes or chocolate items.

Rice Bran: This is the outside layer of the rice kernel which is removed to make brown rice. Contains the bran and part of the rice germ. Found in natural food stores by Ener-G, near the flours or in the baking aisle. Adds important fiber to baked goods. Refrigerate after opening.

Rice Flour: Most common flour used in wheat and gluten-free baking. White rice flour is the rice kernel stripped of most of its nutrients. Brown rice flour contains more layers of the rice kernel—and more nutrients. Store brown rice flour in the refrigerator or freezer to extend shelf life. Found in the baking aisle or bulk sections of natural food stores and some supermarkets. See Wheat-Free Flours in Appendix.

Rice Milk: (Also called rice beverage.) Made from rice, this milk is an effective substitute for cow's milk. Available at natural food stores or supermarkets in liquid or powdered form (which must be reconstituted with water before using). Refrigerate liquid version after opening or reconstituting. Choose enriched or fortified versions. Celiacs must avoid those with brown rice syrup or malted cereal extract (which may contain barley). See Baking with Dairy Substitutes in Appendix.

Rice Polish: Portion of brown rice kernel removed in the process of making white rice. Contains part of the rice germ and bran—high in fiber. Refrigerate after opening. Found in Ener-G box in the baking aisles of natural food stores.

Safflower Oil: Made from the safflower plant, this oil works well in baking or sautéing because of its relatively high smoke point (it won't burn as quickly). Found in baking aisle of supermarkets and natural food stores.

Salt: Use your favorite salt, but check the fillers that make them free-flowing. You may reduce the salt in recipes to suit your individual taste and dietary needs. I use sea salt.

Sour Cream Alternative: Made from soy and performs like real sour cream. Found in dairy section of natural food stores. Some brands contain casein.

Soy Flour: Derived from soy beans, this yellowish-tan flour is found in regular and lower-fat form—usually in the flour section of natural food stores. Refrigerate to avoid rancidity due to fat content. Works best in baked goods with fruit such as carrot cakes. Persons who are allergic to legumes should avoid this flour. See Wheat-Free Flours in Appendix.

Soy Margarine or Oleo: Available at natural food stores. Contains partially hydrogenated soybean oil and must be refrigerated. Legume-allergic persons should avoid. Soy margarine may be used in place of vegetable shortening, butter, or canola oil spread in baking.

Soy Milk: (Also called soy beverage.) Available at natural food stores or supermarkets in liquid or powdered form (which must be reconstituted with water before using and is somewhat lighter in color). Liquid form must be refrigerated after opening or reconstituting. Read labels to avoid problem ingredients. See Baking with Dairy Substitutes in Appendix for guidelines on using soy milk to replace cow's milk.

Soy Sauce: Look for wheat-free tamari versions by Eden and San J. May use Bragg's Amino Acids, which is non-fermented soy sauce without wheat and yeast.

Stevia: A sweet-leafed herb from Paraguay. Sold in powder (green or white), liquid, or leaf form. Slight licorice-like flavor that is perceptible in bland foods, but less noticeable in more strongly flavored dishes such as spice cakes.

Sucanat®: Dried cane juice with water removed. Coarse amber granules impart a mild molasses taste. Available in natural food stores in pre-packaged form in the baking aisle or in bulk form. See Baking with Alternative Sweeteners in Appendix for more information.

Sugar: Bleached or unbleached cane sugar may be used. Beet sugar may also be used. Sugar in some breads in this book may be reduced or eliminated.

Sun-Dried Tomatoes: Dehydrated tomatoes which are packaged dry or packed in oil. Choose the dry packaged version if the source of the oil is uncertain or inappropriate.

Sweet Rice Flour: Derived from short grain rice, this white powder produces baked goods that are more moist and firm than if "long-grain" rice flour is used. Sometimes called "sticky" or "glutinous" rice, it *does not* contain wheat gluten. Sold in boxes by Ener-G in baking aisle or near flours in natural food stores. See Wheat-Free Flours in Appendix.

Tapioca Flour: Made from the cassava plant, this is a fine, white flour that adds chewiness and elasticity to baked goods. Sold in natural food stores in packages or bulk form. See Wheat-Free Flours in Appendix.

Tofu: Be sure to use the soft silken version (made by Mori-Nu®) in baked goods (unless otherwise specified). Store the 10.5 ounce aseptic packages on pantry shelf until opened. Then refrigerate in closed container and use within two days. Found in natural food stores in refrigerated section or in displays near the baking aisle.

Tomato Paste and Tomato Sauce: Contadina makes gluten-free versions of both. However, the tomato sauce also contains corn syrup. Make your own (See page 146).

Vanilla Extract: Many brands contain alcohol (which may be wheat or gluten-based). Look for those that are alcohol-free. See **Extracts or Flavorings** in this chapter. See Mail Order Sources in Appendix.

Vanilla Powder: Derived from vanilla beans, this white powder may also have sugar added. Powdered vanilla bean is dark brown in color. Both are available by mail order from companies that sell flavorings and extracts. Powders may be used interchangeably with liquid vanilla extract, but may need to add a teaspoon of water to restore moisture to the batter or dough. See Mail Order Sources in Appendix.

Vinegar: Be sure to use cider or wine vinegar, which are wheat and gluten-free. Distilled vinegar may be grain-based. Make sure the cider vinegar is not just distilled vinegar with apple flavoring. Use Ener-G yeast-free/gluten-free vinegar if yeast and fermentation are problems. This powder must be reconstituted with water before using and then refrigerated. Made from acetic acid and maltodextrin from corn.

Vitamin C Crystals or Powder: Derived from the fermentation of corn, this powder adds acid to yeast dough and strengthens the protein structure. Also acts as acid leavening component in non-yeast breads which are baked in the oven, not in a bread machine. Sold in supplement sections of natural food stores. Make sure the jar says it's wheat and gluten-free. Choose unbuffered Vitamin C or it will not add acid to the bread.

Yeast: Choose gluten-free yeast such as Red Star or the Gluten-Free Pantry's SAF. In this book, dry yeast is the term used to indicate regular yeast.

Yogurt: If you can use cow's milk, look for yogurts with no tapioca or modified food starch. Dannon and Land O'Lakes are gluten-free and have good acidolphilus content. Look for lactose-reduced yogurt. Milk-allergic people should not use goat's milk yogurt, but milk-intolerant people seem to do fine with it. Soy yogurt does not work in baking.

Xanthan gum: Derived from bacteria in corn sugar, this gum lends structure and texture to baked goods and can thicken sauces. Probably the most indispensable ingredient when baking without wheat or gluten. Found in the baking aisle or near flours in natural food stores. Seems expensive, but lasts a long time since only a tiny amount is used in recipes.

Water: Some cooks insist that using filtered water instead of tap water produces a sweeter, fuller flavor in baked goods. Feel free to use the water of your choice.

BREADS

Here is bread, which strengthens man's heart, and therefore called the staff of life. — Matthew Henry

B read is the staff of life. Ask most people on a wheat-free or gluten-free diet what dish they miss the most and they're likely to reply "bread".

Just try the wonderful, flavorful bread recipes in this chapter and a whole new world of breads opens up. You can have sandwiches, hamburger buns, and even a fantastic pizza. In fact, these recipes are so good that you can serve them to anyone—whether they're on special diets or not. And they might not know the difference!

The first section in this chapter features breads and flatbreads leavened with yeast. If your diet excludes yeast, see page 31 for a special section on yeast-free breads and flatbreads. Each recipe is designed to suit the typical wheat or gluten-free diet, but additional suggestions are offered for further customizing each bread so it is appropriate for people who must also exclude eggs, dairy products, or refined sugar from their diets.

One important note: all the "hand methods" for yeast breads use a single rather than double rising which should considerably shorten your preparation time. If you're using a programmable bread machine, you may want to program it for one rise. However, if you prefer two risings, then continue with that procedure. See page 27 for more details.

See page 9 for information on the special ingredients used in these recipes.

See the Breakfast Breads & Dishes chapter
for muffins, scones, biscuits, and so on

PIZZA CRUST

(can be made without wheat, gluten, dairy, or eggs - see page 9 about ingredients)

This crispy pizza crust tastes so delicious that your guests won't know it's wheat and gluten-free. You can hold a slice in your hand and it won't crumble! You may also shape the dough into 4 individual pizzas. Use your favorite toppings, but if you need suggestions for avoiding dairy and tomatoes, see page 21. You'll find a fantastic, easy, fat-free Pizza Sauce in the Salad Dressings and Sauces chapter.

1　tablespoon gluten-free dry yeast
2/3　cup brown rice flour or bean flour
　　(from Authentic Foods)
1/2　cup tapioca flour
2　tablespoons dry milk powder or non-
　　dairy milk powder*
2　teaspoons xanthan gum
1/2　teaspoon salt

1　teaspoon unflavored gelatin powder
1　teaspoon Italian herb seasoning
2/3　cup warm water (105°)
1/2　teaspoon sugar or 1/4 teaspoon honey
1　teaspoon olive oil
1　teaspoon cider vinegar or 1/4 teaspoon
　　unbuffered Vitamin C crystals
cooking spray

Preheat oven to 425 degrees.

In medium mixer bowl using regular beaters (not dough hooks), blend the yeast, flours, dry milk powder, xanthan gum, salt, gelatin powder, and Italian herb seasoning on low speed. Add warm water, sugar (or honey), olive oil, and vinegar. Beat on high speed for 3 minutes. (If the mixer bounces around the bowl, the dough is too stiff. Add water if necessary, one tablespoon at a time, until dough does not resist beaters.) The dough will resemble soft bread dough. (You may also mix in bread machine on dough setting.)

Put mixture into 12-inch pizza pan or on baking sheet (for thin, crispy crust), 11 x 7-inch pan (for deep dish version) that has been coated with cooking spray. Liberally sprinkle rice flour onto dough, then press dough into pan, continuing to sprinkle dough with flour to prevent sticking to your hands. Make edges thicker to contain the toppings.

Bake the pizza crust for 10 minutes. Remove from oven. Spread pizza crust with your favorite sauce and toppings. Bake for another 20-25 minutes or until top is nicely browned.

Preparation = 45 minutes. Serves 6.

| Crust Only: | | | | | | | | Exchanges | | |
Calories	Fat	% Fat Cal	Protein	Carbohydrate	Cholesterol	Sodium	Fiber	Carbohydrate	Meat	Fat
138	1 g	8 %	2 g	30 g	0 mg	286 mg	2 g	2		1/4

*Dairy Alternative: 2 tablespoons tapioca flour or sweet rice flour in place of the 2 tablespoons dry milk powder or non-dairy milk powder. However, the crust won't brown as nicely.

See next page for Pizza Tips and page 42 for a Yeast-Free Pizza Crust.

TIPS FOR THE PERFECT PIZZA

Pizza Pans

Use nonstick, non-insulated metal pans for best results. Perforated pizza pans are not recommended for the first 10 minutes of baking because the unbaked dough falls through the perforations. However, once the pizza crust has baked for 10 minutes (prior to placing the toppings on it), you may slide the crust onto a perforated pan and continue baking as directed. Also, perforated pans work fine for re-heating a whole pizza or pizza slices.

Some people have success using baking stones; others do not. The problem is that the wet, sticky dough tends to stick to the stone, making cleanup difficult. If you're determined to use the stone, sprinkle with cornmeal first or use parchment paper. Also, rather than patting the dough onto a preheated stone and burning yourself, pat it onto a cold stone. Then place in preheated oven. You'll need a peel (flat, wide wooden "spatula") to remove the pizza from the stone or some stones have built-in carriers. The stone will be very hot.

Another idea is to bake the pizza on a nonstick pan for the first 10 minutes. Remove from the oven, top with toppings, and slide it onto a heated pizza stone in the oven. Once again, a wooden peel will reduce the chances of burned fingers.

Wood-Fired or Grilled Pizzas

Yes, you can cook this pizza on a grill—just like in the restaurants! Bake the crust on a pizza pan in the oven for 10 minutes, as directed on the previous page. Top with toppings and transfer to a barbecue grill using large spatulas or a wooden peel, if you have one. I use a gas grill with two temperature controls, and I place the pizza over low heat on one side and keep the other side about medium temperature. Close the lid and cook (peeking occasionally) for about 10 minutes, or until cheese is melted. The cheese won't brown as much as it would in the oven because there is no direct heat from above.

Freezing

You may freeze the pizza crust after it has baked for 10 minutes. Or, freeze the entire pizza after it has been topped with your favorite toppings and baked for 20 minutes. Be sure to cool thoroughly, then wrap tightly with aluminum foil before placing in the freezer. Some people prepare several pizza crusts, bake them for 10 minutes and then freeze them, using them like the commercial pizza crusts you find in supermarkets. Defrost in the refrigerator or in microwave (however, micro-waving may produce a slightly soggy crust).

Storing Leftovers

Leftover pizza may be frozen (see Freezing above). Or, wrap cooled pizza tightly and store in refrigerator for up to 2 days. Re-heat in oven on pizza pan or perforated pizza pan.

PIZZA MIX

(can be made without wheat, gluten, dairy, or eggs - see page 9 about ingredients)

Keep this mix on hand and you can have pizza in no time at all. It makes 4 pizzas.

2 2/3 cups brown rice flour
2 cups tapioca flour
1/2 cup dry milk powder or non-dairy
    milk powder or 1/2 cup sweet rice flour

4 teaspoons xanthan gum
2 teaspoons salt
4 teaspoons unflavored gelatin powder
4 teaspoons Italian herb seasoning

Combine all ingredients in airtight container and store in dark, dry place. To make one 12-inch pizza, place 1 1/3 cups of the dry mixture in a medium bowl. Add 1 tablespoon gluten-free dry yeast, 2/3 cup warm water (105°), 1/2 teaspoon sugar (or 1/4 teaspoon honey), 1 teaspoon olive oil and 1 teaspoon cider vinegar (or 1/4 teaspoon unbuffered Vitamin C crystals).

Mix with electric mixer on high speed for 3 minutes. Follow directions for Pizza Crust on page 19. (Or use your bread machine to mix the dough on dough setting.)

Dairy-Free, Tomato-Free, Pesto Pizza

Bake Pizza Crust at 425 degrees for 10 minutes. Remove from oven. Brush Pizza Crust with 3/4 cup pesto. (Use commercial pesto or make your own with recipe on page 135.) Then top with your choice of vegetables (I use a total of 2 cups of chopped mushrooms, chopped black olives, diced onion, red bell pepper, etc., all sautéed together in a skillet over medium heat until limp.) Bake for 15-20 minutes or until desired doneness.

Preparation = 45 minutes. Serves 6.

Topping Only								Exchanges		
Calories	Fat	% Fat Cal	Protein	Carbohydrate	Cholesterol	Sodium	Fiber	Carbohydrate	Meat	Fat
260	23 g	77 %	8 g	7 mg	13 mg	458 mg	1 g	1/2		5

Sun-Dried Tomato & Olive Pizza

Bake Pizza Crust at 425 degrees for 10 minutes. Top crust with 1/2 cup chopped sun dried tomatoes, 1/2 cup chopped black olives, and 1-2 teaspoons of dried oregano or basil (to taste). Bake at 425 degrees for 15-20 minutes.

Preparation = 45 minutes. Serves 6.

Topping Only								Exchanges		
Calories	Fat	% Fat Cal	Protein	Carbohydrate	Cholesterol	Sodium	Fiber	Carbohydrate	Meat	Fat
250	22 g	77 %	8 g	7 g	13 mg	454 mg	1 g	1/2		4

NOTE: See page 42 for a yeast-free pizza crust. Also, two ounces of feta cheese (made from goat's milk) makes a tasty addition to any of these pizzas—if it is appropriate for your diet.

FOCACCIA

(can be made without wheat, gluten, or dairy - see page 9 about ingredients)

Focaccia is a cross between pizza and rustic Italian flat bread. It's very easy to make and the dough is especially forgiving. The pan size determines the shape and thickness of the bread.

1 1/2 teaspoons gluten-free dry yeast
1 cup brown rice flour*
1/4 cup potato starch
1/4 cup tapioca flour
1 1/2 teaspoons xanthan gum
1 teaspoon unflavored gelatin powder
1 teaspoon dried rosemary
1/2 teaspoon onion powder
3/4 teaspoon salt
3/4 cup warm water (105°)
1 teaspoon sugar or 1/2 teaspoon honey

2 large eggs
2 tablespoons olive oil
1/2 teaspoon cider vinegar

TOPPING
1 tablespoon olive oil
1 1/4 teaspoons Italian herb seasoning
1/4 teaspoon kosher or coarse sea salt (you
   may also use table salt, if you wish)
cooking spray

Combine yeast, flours, xanthan gum, gelatin powder, rosemary, onion powder, and 3/4 teaspoon of salt in a small mixer bowl. Add warm water, sugar (or honey), eggs, 2 tablespoons olive oil, and vinegar. Beat dough with mixer (using regular beaters, not dough hooks) for 2 minutes. The dough will be soft and sticky—like thick cake batter. (You may also mix this dough in your bread machine on "dough" setting.)

Transfer dough to 11 x 7-inch nonstick pan, 8-inch round nonstick pan, or 15 x 10-inch nonstick pan that has been sprayed with cooking spray. Cover with aluminum foil and let rise in warm place for 30 minutes or until desired height.

Preheat oven to 400 degrees. Sprinkle Focaccia with 1 tablespoon of olive oil (or to taste), 1 1/4 teaspoons Italian herb seasoning and 1/4 teaspoon salt. Bake for 15 minutes or until top is golden brown. You may drizzle additional olive oil on baked Focaccia, if you wish. (A sprinkle of Parmesan cheese is optional.) Makes one 8-inch or 11 x 7-inch or one 15 x 10-inch loaf.

Preparation = 1 hour. Serves 6.

| | | | | | | | | Exchanges | | |
Calories	Fat	% Fat Cal	Protein	Carbohydrate	Cholesterol	Sodium	Fiber	Carbohydrate	Meat	Fat
250	9 g	32 %	4 g	40 g	60 mg	379 mg	2 g	2 3/4		2

*Flour Alternative: 1 cup bean flour (from Authentic Foods) in place of 1 cup brown rice flour

See page 23 for Focaccia toppings and page 43 for Yeast-Free Focaccia.

FOCACCIA TOPPINGS

HERB: Combine 1/2 teaspoon dried rosemary, 1/2 teaspoon dried sage, 1/2 teaspoon dried thyme, 1/4 teaspoon black pepper, and 2 tablespoons Parmesan cheese. Sprinkle on top. Bake as directed. Serves 6.

Topping Only | | | | | | | | Exchanges | |
Calories	Fat	% Fat Cal	Protein	Carbohydrate	Cholesterol	Sodium	Fiber	Carbohydrate	Meat	Fat
10	<1 g	54 %	1 g	<1 g	1 mg	30 mg	<1 g		1/4 L	1/4

SUN-DRIED TOMATO, OLIVE, AND PESTO: 1/4 cup chopped sun-dried tomatoes, 1/4 cup chopped black olives, and 1/4 cup chopped onion sautéed until translucent in 1 teaspoon olive oil. Use Pesto recipe on page 135. Top Focaccia dough with tomatoes, olives, onion, and pesto. Bake as directed. Serves 6.

Topping Only | | | | | | | | Exchanges | |
Calories	Fat	% Fat Cal	Protein	Carbohydrate	Cholesterol	Sodium	Fiber	Carbohydrate	Meat	Fat
170	15 g	77 %	5 g	4 g	9 mg	300 mg	1 g		2 L	4 1/2

CARAMELIZED ONION: Sprinkle Focaccia dough with 1-2 teaspoons dried oregano, thyme, or herb of choice. Then top with 2 cups of chopped, sautéed onions that have been tossed with 1 tablespoon olive oil. Bake as directed. Serves 6.

Topping Only | | | | | | | | Exchanges | |
Calories	Fat	% Fat Cal	Protein	Carbohydrate	Cholesterol	Sodium	Fiber	Carbohydrate	Meat	Fat
42	2 g	50 %	<1 g	5 g	0 mg	2 mg	1 g	1/4		3/4

Focaccia Pizza: You can top Focaccia with any of your favorite toppings for a Focaccia pizza.

HERBED FLATBREAD

(can be made without wheat, gluten, dairy, or eggs - see page 9 about ingredients)

This is very easy to make and the dough is very forgiving. Vary the seeds as you wish.

1 tablespoon gluten-free dry yeast
2/3 cup brown rice flour or bean flour (from Authentic Foods)
1/2 cup tapioca flour
2 tablespoons dry milk powder or non-dairy milk powder*
2 teaspoons xanthan gum
1/2 teaspoon salt
1 teaspoon instant minced onion
1/2 teaspoon each caraway seeds, dill seeds, cumin seeds, mustard seeds, and fennel seeds

1/2 teaspoon sugar or 1/4 teaspoon honey
2/3 warm water (105°)
1 teaspoon olive oil
1 teaspoon cider vinegar or 1/4 teaspoon unbuffered Vitamin C crystals

TOPPING
1 tablespoon olive oil or cooking spray
1/2 teaspoon kosher or coarse salt
cooking spray (for pan)

In medium mixer bowl using regular beaters (not dough hooks), blend the yeast, flours, dry milk powder, xanthan gum, salt, onion, seeds, and sugar (or honey) on low speed. Add warm water, olive oil and vinegar. Beat on high speed for 3 minutes. (If the mixer bounces around the bowl, the dough is too dry. Add water if necessary, one tablespoon at a time, until dough does not resist beaters.) The dough should resemble soft bread dough.

Preheat oven to 400 degrees. Place dough on 15 x 10-inch pan that has been coated with cooking spray. Liberally sprinkle rice flour on dough, then press dough into pan with hands, continuing to sprinkle dough with rice flour to prevent sticking to your hands. Dough should extend up to within 1 inch of pan edge, but should not touch edge of pan.

Brush with olive oil or—if you're watching calories—you may spray with cooking spray. Sprinkle with salt.

Bake for 15-20 minutes or golden brown and edges are turned up. Remove from oven. Cut or tear into pieces.

Preparation = 25 minutes. Serves 6.

Per piece:

| | | | | | | | | Exchanges | | |
Calories	Fat	% Fat Cal	Protein	Carbohydrate	Cholesterol	Sodium	Fiber	Carbohydrate	Meat	Fat
138	1 g	8 %	2 g	30 g	0 mg	192 mg	1 g	2		1/4

*Dairy Alternative: You may use 2 tablespoons tapioca flour or sweet rice flour in place of the dry milk powder or non-dairy powder. However, the bread won't brown as nicely.

SANDWICH BREAD

(can be made without wheat, gluten, or dairy - see page 9 about ingredients)

You'll want to keep a loaf of this bread on hand at all times because you'll use it so often—for sandwiches, toast, bread crumbs, and so on. Note the different amounts of yeast for the hand versus bread machine versions. Ingredients should be room temperature, unless otherwise noted.

gluten-free dry yeast (see specific instructions)
1 cup water (see specific instructions)
2 tablespoons sugar or 3 teaspoons honey
1 1/2 cups white or brown rice flour
1/2 cup potato starch
1/4 cup tapioca flour
2 teaspoons xanthan gum
1 teaspoon salt
1/4 teaspoon soy lecithin granules

1/3 cup dry milk powder or non-dairy milk powder or sweet rice flour
1 teaspoon Ener-G Egg Replacer powder
2 large eggs at room temperature
3 tablespoons melted butter or cooking oil
1 teaspoon cider vinegar or 1/4 teaspoon unbuffered Vitamin C crystals
cooking spray

HAND METHOD: Make sure all ingredients are at room temperature. Combine **1 tablespoon dry yeast**, 2 teaspoons of the sugar (or all of the honey), and the water (105°). Set aside until foamy, about 5 minutes.

In large mixer bowl using regular beaters (not dough hooks), combine flours, xanthan gum, salt, remainder of sugar, lecithin, dry milk powder, and Egg Replacer. Add eggs, melted butter (or oil), vinegar, and yeast mixture.

Mix ingredients together on low speed until liquid is incorporated, then increase mixer speed to high and beat for 2 minutes. Occasionally, scrape sides of bowl with spatula.

For smaller loaves, coat three small pans, 5 x 2 1/2-inches, with cooking spray. Divide dough among pans, smooth tops with spatula, and put in warm place to rise for 35-40 minutes or until doubled in bulk.

For one large loaf, use 9 x 5-inch nonstick pan coated with cooking spray. Place dough in pan, smooth top with spatula, and let dough rise in warm place until double in bulk, 35-40 minutes.

Preheat oven to 350 degrees. Bake small loaves for 25-30 minutes, large loaf for 40-50 minutes or until nicely browned. Cool 5 minutes in pan, then remove from pan and cool on wire rack.

BREAD MACHINE: Use **1 1/2 teaspoons of yeast**. Follow bread machine instructions, making sure kneading blade is in place. (See page 27 for programming times.) Spray pan with cooking spray. I combine dry ingredients and add to bread machine. Combine liquid ingredients (eggs should be whisked thoroughly; all ingredients should be at room temperature, including water at 80°). Pour carefully over dry ingredients in bread machine. Set controls and bake. Makes a 1-pound loaf.

Preparation = 3 hours by machine (depending on machine); 2 hours by hand. Serves 10.

| | | | | | | | | Exchanges | | |
Calories	Fat	% Fat Cal	Protein	Carbohydrate	Cholesterol	Sodium	Fiber	Carbohydrate	Meat	Fat
190	5 g	24 %	5 g	31 g	46 mg	281 mg	<1 g	2		1

PUMPERNICKEL BREAD

(can be made without wheat, gluten, or dairy - see page 9 about ingredients)

This bread is thick, dense, and filling. It makes great sandwiches—try it in your next Reuben. Note the smaller yeast amount for the bread machine version.

gluten-free dry yeast (see specific instructions)
1 cup water (see specific instructions)
2 tablespoons brown sugar*
1 cup brown rice flour
1/2 cup potato starch
1/2 cup tapioca flour
3 teaspoons caraway seeds
2 teaspoons flax seeds (optional)
1 teaspoon instant coffee powder
1/2 teaspoon onion powder
2 teaspoons xanthan gum

1 teaspoon unflavored gelatin powder
1 teaspoon salt
6 tablespoons dry milk powder**
2 teaspoons Ener-G Egg Replacer powder
1 tablespoon cocoa or carob powder
2 large eggs at room temperature
2 tablespoons canola, safflower, or other oil
2 tablespoons molasses
1 teaspoon cider vinegar or 1/4 teaspoon unbuffered Vitamin C crystals
cooking spray

HAND METHOD: Make sure all ingredients are at room temperature. Combine **1 tablespoon yeast**, 2 teaspoons of the brown sugar, and warm water (105°) in small bowl. Set aside to foam for 5 minutes.

In large mixer bowl using regular beaters (not dough hooks), combine flours, seeds, coffee powder, onion powder, xanthan gum, gelatin powder, salt dry milk powder, Egg Replacer, and cocoa. Add eggs, oil, molasses, vinegar, and yeast mixture.

Mix ingredients together on low speed until liquid is incorporated, then increase mixer speed to high and beat for 2 minutes. Occasionally, scrape sides of bowl with spatula.

For small loaves, coat three 5 x 2 1/2-inch nonstick loaf pans with cooking spray. Divide dough among pans, smooth tops with spatula, and put in warm place to rise for 35-40 minutes or until doubled.

For a large loaf, use 9 x 5-inch nonstick pan coated with cooking spray. Place dough in pan, smooth top with spatula and let rise in warm place until doubled, about 35-40 minutes.

Preheat oven to 350 degrees. Bake small loaves for 25-30 minutes, large loaf for 40-50 minutes, or until nicely browned. Cool 5 minutes; remove from pan. Cool on wire rack.

BREAD MACHINE: Use **1 1/2 teaspoons yeast**. Follow machine instructions. I combine dry ingredients and add to bread machine. Combine liquid ingredients. (Eggs should be whisked thoroughly; all ingredients should be at room temperature, including water at 80°.) Pour carefully over dry ingredients in bread machine. Set controls and bake. (See page 27 for programming times.) Makes a 1-pound loaf.

Preparation = 3 hours. Serves 10.

								Exchanges		
Calories	Fat	% Fat Cal	Protein	Carbohydrate	Cholesterol	Sodium	Fiber	Carbohydrate	Meat	Fat
185	4 g	21 %	5 g	32 g	37 mg	245 mg	2 g	2 1/2		1

See next page for dairy and sugar alternatives.

*Sugar Alternative: Same amount of dried cane juice or maple sugar in place of brown sugar. Or omit brown sugar altogether and increase molasses to 3 tablespoons.

**Dairy Alternative: Use non-dairy milk powder in place of dry milk powder. Or use 6 tablespoons tapioca flour or sweet rice flour to omit dairy altogether.

TIPS FOR FAIL-PROOF YEAST BREAD

General guidelines for making bread with a bread machine:

1. Have all ingredients, including water, at room temperature (about 80°).

2. Follow instructions for *your* bread machine. With some, add dry ingredients first, then liquid. In others, the liquid ingredients come first. Whisk dry ingredients together *thoroughly* before adding to bread machine to assure thorough blending. Whisk liquid ingredients together *thoroughly,* especially the eggs, before adding to bread machine. Some people also mix *all* ingredients together thoroughly before adding to machine.

3. Be careful not to dislodge the kneading blade when scraping the sides of the pan.

4. With programmable machines, some experimentation may be required to achieve the right settings. My Welbilt (on light setting) warms the ingredients for 20 minutes, mixes 10 minutes, rests 5 minutes, kneads 15 minutes, rises 25 minutes, punches down then rises again 54 minutes. It bakes for 40 minutes. Total time is 2 hours and 50 minutes. If you wish to program your machine for one rise, eliminate the second rising of 54 minutes.

5. If the bread falls, there was probably too much liquid. Next time, add all but 2 tablespoons of the water and watch the dough as it kneads. If it looks dry, add water 1 tablespoon at a time. When the dough is the right consistency, it should swirl about in the machine with a visible raised pattern on top.

6. Place the bread machine in a spot that is neither too hot or too cold for best results.

7. To assure easy removal of baked bread, coat insides of pan with cooking spray.

General guidelines for making bread by hand:

1. Have all ingredients, except water, at room temperature (about 80°). Heat water to 105°.

2. Once dough begins to rise in pan, don't disturb the delicate structure by shaking, dropping, or jarring the pan. Don't slam the oven door.

3. Rising times vary by altitude—lower altitudes may take up to 30 minutes longer.

4. Humidity, temperature, and brand of flour may affect the amount of liquid required.

BREADSTICKS

(can be made without wheat, gluten, dairy, or eggs - see page 9 about ingredients)

These breadsticks taste great with a pasta dinner. You can experiment with adding different herbs to the dough or sprinkling the breadsticks with your favorite Italian spices.

1 tablespoon gluten-free dry yeast
1/2 cup brown rice flour or bean flour (from Authentic Foods)
1/2 cup tapioca flour
1 tablespoon dry milk powder or non-dairy milk powder
2 teaspoons xanthan gum
1/2 cup grated Parmesan cheese (cow, rice, or soy)
1/2 teaspoon salt

1 teaspoon onion powder
1 teaspoon unflavored gelatin powder
2/3 cup warm water (105°)
1/2 teaspoon sugar or 1/4 teaspoon honey
1 tablespoon olive oil
1 teaspoon cider vinegar or 1/4 teaspoon unbuffered Vitamin C crystals
1 teaspoon Italian herb seasoning
cooking spray

Preheat oven to 400 degrees for 5 minutes, then turn off.

In medium mixer bowl while oven is preheating, blend the yeast, flours, dry milk powder, xanthan gum, Parmesan cheese, salt, onion powder, and gelatin powder on low speed of electric mixer. Add warm water, sugar (or honey), olive oil, and vinegar. Beat on high for 3 minutes. Dough will be soft and sticky. (Bread machine is not recommended.)

Place dough in large, *heavy-duty* plastic freezer bag that has 1/2-inch opening cut diagonally on one corner. (This makes a 1-inch circle.) Coat a large baking sheet with cooking spray. Squeeze dough out of plastic bag onto sheet in 10 strips, each 1-inch wide by 6 inches long. For best results, hold the bag of dough upright as you squeeze, rather than at an angle. Spray breadsticks with cooking spray, then sprinkle with herb seasoning.

Place in warmed oven to rise for 20-30 minutes. Leaving breadsticks in oven, turn oven to 400 degrees and bake until golden brown, about 15-20 minutes. Switch position of cookie sheet halfway through baking to assure even browning. Cool on wire rack. When cool, store in airtight container.

Preparation Time = 1 hour, 15 minutes. Serves 10 (one breadstick each).

Per breadstick: Exchanges

Calories	Fat	% Fat Cal	Protein	Carbohydrate	Cholesterol	Sodium	Fiber	Carbohydrate	Meat	Fat
110	3 g	23 g	3 g	18 g	3 g	260	<1 g	1	1/2 L	1/2

*Dairy Alternative: Omit dry milk powder altogether. If you omit milk powder <u>and</u> Parmesan, increase tapioca flour to 3/4 cup. There will be some loss of taste and texture when Parmesan cheese is omitted.

HAMBURGER BUNS

(can be made without wheat, gluten, or dairy - see page 9 about ingredients)

Serve these buns at your next picnic and everyone will love them. They're flavorful, won't crumble. and have a marvelous texture. If you don't have English muffin rings (available at kitchen stores) use 8 ounce pineapple cans with ends removed. Or see below for aluminum foil rings.

1 1/2 teaspoons gluten-free dry yeast
1 teaspoon sugar or 1/2 teaspoon honey
1 cup brown rice flour*
1/4 cup potato starch
1/4 cup tapioca flour
1 1/2 teaspoons xanthan gum
1 teaspoon unflavored gelatin powder
1 tablespoon instant minced onion
3/4 teaspoon salt
1/4 teaspoon soy lecithin granules
3/4 cup warm water (105°)
2 tablespoons canola, safflower, or other oil
2 large eggs
1/2 teaspoon cider vinegar or 1/4 teaspoon unbuffered Vitamin C crystals

Combine yeast, sugar, flours, xanthan gum, gelatin powder, onion, salt, and lecithin in a small mixer bowl. Add warm water, oil, eggs, and vinegar to the flour mixture. Beat dough with electric mixer (using regular beaters, not dough hooks) for 2 minutes. The dough will be soft and sticky. (Or mix in bread machine on dough setting.)

Transfer dough to eight English muffin rings on baking sheet. Rings and sheet should be coated with cooking spray. Cover with aluminum foil and let rise in warm place for 30 minutes or until desired height.

Preheat oven to 400 degrees. Bake for 15-20 minutes or until tops are golden brown. Cool 5 minutes, then remove buns from rings. Lightly toasting the cut side of bun before serving produces a crispy texture. Makes 8 buns.

Preparation = 1 hour. Serves 8.

Per bun:

Calories	Fat	% Fat Cal	Protein	Carbohydrate	Cholesterol	Sodium	Fiber	Exchanges Carbohydrate	Exchanges Meat	Exchanges Fat
170	5 g	26 %	3 g	29 g	45 mg	290 mg	1 g	2		1

***Flour Alternative:** 1 cup bean flour (from Authentic Foods) in place of 1 cup brown rice flour

Variation: For an herb-flavored bun, add 1 teaspoon rosemary leaves (crushed) and 1/2 teaspoon Italian herb seasoning to the dough.

Aluminum Foil Rings: Fold a 12-inch strip of regular-size aluminum foil lengthwise into a 1-inch wide strip. Secure ends together with masking tape to form ring.

YEAST-FREE BREADS

Give us this day our daily bread. —Matthew 6:2

For some people, it is not only the wheat or gluten in bread that causes a problem—it is also the yeast! However, there are other ways to leaven breads without using yeast.

In this section, you'll find several breads that can be used for sandwiches or to accompany main dishes at dinner time. You won't even miss the yeast, because these breads are tasty and have a great texture and appearance.

Yeast-Free Breads

Yeast-Free Flatbreads

For yeast-free breakfast breads, see the Breakfast Breads & Dishes chapter.

See page 9 for information on the special ingredients used in these recipes.

YEAST-FREE HAMBURGER BUNS #1

(can be made without wheat, gluten, dairy, eggs, or refined sugar - see page 9 about ingredients)

Use these buns for hamburgers and sandwiches—or lightly toast them for breakfast. They have a slight buttery onion taste, but you can also substitute your favorite herbs and spices, if you wish. And, they won't crumble! If you use the butter extract, you may need to add extra salt. You may omit the sugar, if you wish.

- 1 cup brown or white rice flour
- 2/3 cup potato starch
- 1/3 cup tapioca flour
- 2 teaspoons sugar or 1/2 teaspoon honey
- 2 teaspoons xanthan gum
- 3/4 teaspoon salt
- 1/2 teaspoon unflavored gelatin powder
- 1/4 teaspoon soy lecithin granules
- 1 teaspoon baking powder

- 1 1/4 teaspoons baking soda
- 1 tablespoon instant minced onion
- 1 teaspoon Butter Buds or gluten-free butter extract
- 2 large eggs or 2 teaspoons Ener-G Egg Replacer powder dissolved in 1/3 cup water
- 1 cup milk (cow, rice, soy, or nut)
- 2 tablespoons canola, safflower, or other oil
- 2 teaspoons sesame seeds (optional)

Preheat oven to 375 degrees. Spray eight 4-inch English muffin or aluminum foil rings on nonstick baking pan with cooking spray. (See page 29 for making aluminum foil rings.) Combine dry ingredients in large mixing bowl. With electric mixer on low, add eggs (or reconstituted Egg Replacer), milk, and oil to bowl and blend on medium speed for 2 minutes. Dough will be soft and sticky.

Spoon into eight prepared rings and smooth tops with wet spatula, if necessary. Sprinkle with sesame seeds, if using. Bake for 15-20 minutes or until tops are lightly browned. (For extra large buns, make your own aluminum foil rings in desired size or make smaller rings for luncheons or cocktail parties.)

Preparation = 30 minutes. Makes 8 buns.

Per bun:

Calories	Fat	% Fat Cal	Protein	Carbohydrate	Cholesterol	Sodium	Fiber	Carbohydrate	Meat	Fat
200	6 g	28 %	5 g	31 g	27 mg	478 mg	1 g	2		1 1/4

Note: If you make your own aluminum foil rings, you can control the size of the buns. Also, the aluminum foil rings won't scratch your nonstick pans. Or bake the buns in 10-ounce glass baking cups.

YEAST-FREE HAMBURGER BUNS #2

(can be made without wheat, gluten, dairy, eggs, or refined sugar - see page 9 about ingredients)

This recipe uses tofu instead of eggs to bind the ingredients together. Due to the tofu, the buns won't brown as thoroughly as version #1 on the previous page. However, the bun is nicely textured and moist. If you use the butter extract, you may need to increase the salt slightly. You may omit the sugar, if you wish.

1 cup boiling water
1/2 cup soft silken tofu by Mori-Nu®
1 cup brown or white rice flour
2/3 cup potato starch
1/3 cup tapioca flour
2 teaspoons sugar or 1/2 teaspoon honey
2 teaspoons xanthan gum
3/4 teaspoon salt
1/2 teaspoon unflavored gelatin powder

1/2 teaspoon soy lecithin granules
1 teaspoon baking powder
1 1/4 teaspoons baking soda
1 tablespoon instant minced onion
1 teaspoon butter-flavored salt or gluten-free butter extract
3 tablespoons canola, safflower, or other oil
2 teaspoons sesame seeds (optional)

Preheat oven to 375 degrees. Coat eight 4-inch English muffins or aluminum foil rings on nonstick baking pan with cooking spray. (See page 29 for making aluminum foil rings.)

Combine boiling water and tofu in food processor and puree until very, very smooth. Add remaining ingredients (except sesame seeds) and mix thoroughly. Dough will be soft and sticky.

Spoon dough into prepared rings and smooth tops with wet spatula, if necessary. Sprinkle with sesame seeds, if using. Bake for 15-20 minutes or until tops are firm and begin to split. Tops will not brown as thoroughly due to tofu.

Remove buns from rings. Cool completely on wire rack before slicing horizontally with serrated knife or electric knife. (You can make smaller aluminum rings for daintier buns.)

Preparation = 30 minutes. Serves 8.

Per bun:

Calories	Fat	% Fat Cal	Protein	Carbohydrate	Cholesterol	Sodium	Fiber	Exchanges Carbohydrate	Meat	Fat
215	6 g	23 %	3 g	40 g	0 mg	458 mg	1 g	3		1 1/4

YEAST-FREE SANDWICH BREAD

(can be made without wheat, gluten, dairy, or refined sugar - see page 9 about ingredients)

If you're craving bread but can't have yeast—this is the recipe for you. It produces a firm, dense bread that is perfect for sandwiches and makes wonderful toast or bread crumbs. This version produces a higher, lighter bread than the egg-free version (below), which is heavier and more dense. You may omit the sugar, if you wish.

1 cup brown or white rice flour (or bean flour from Authentic Foods)
2/3 cup potato starch
1/3 cup tapioca flour
1 teaspoon sugar or honey
2 teaspoons xanthan gum
3/4 teaspoon Butter Buds, butter-flavored salt, or regular salt

1/2 teaspoon unflavored gelatin powder
1/2 teaspoon cream of tartar
1/2 teaspoon baking soda
1 large egg, lightly beaten
1 1/3 cups non-fat plain yogurt*
2 tablespoons melted butter or canola, safflower, or other oil
cooking spray

Coat two 5 x 2 1/2-inch nonstick pans (or 8 x 4-inch nonstick pan) with cooking spray. This bread can also be baked in a 7-inch round casserole, but it slices better for sandwiches in the rectangular pans. Preheat oven to 375 degrees.

Combine dry ingredients in large mixing bowl and mix well. With electric mixer on low, add remaining ingredients and blend on medium speed for 2 minutes.

Spoon into prepared pans, smooth tops with wet spatula (if necessary), and bake small pans for 45-50 minutes, large pan for 50-55 minutes or until top is deeply browned and loaf sounds hollow when tapped. Don't underbake. Cool on wire rack. Slice with serrated knife or electric knife when bread reaches room temperature.

Preparation = 1 1/4 hours. Serves 8.

Per slice: Exchanges

Calories	Fat	% Fat Cal	Protein	Carbohydrate	Cholesterol	Sodium	Fiber	Carbohydrate	Meat	Fat
215	5 g	19 %	5 g	40 g	23 mg	318 mg	1 g	3		1

*Dairy Alternative: 1 cup milk (rice, soy, or nut) in place of 1 1/3 cups yogurt

Yeast-Free Sandwich Bread Without Eggs: Omit egg. Add 2 teaspoons Ener-G Egg Replacer and 1/4 cup water. Increase cream of tartar and baking soda to 1 teaspoon each. Bake as directed. Cool completely before slicing with serrated knife or electric knife.

Yeast-Free Dill-Onion Bread: Omit caraway seeds and add 1 teaspoon dill weed and 1 1/2 tablespoons dill seed or to taste.

Other Variations: Tailor this basic bread to suit your individual tastes and dietary needs. For more fiber, add sesame seeds, rice bran, or rice polish and subtract an equivalent amount of rice flour. For additional flavor, add 1 tablespoon minced onion. For herb bread, add 1-2 teaspoons (or more, to taste) of your favorite dried herbs or spices.

IRISH SODA BREAD

(can be made without wheat, gluten, dairy, or refined sugar - see page 9 about ingredients)

This is the classic soda bread. And it's very quick and easy because you don't have to let it rise like a yeast bread. Use it for sandwiches or to accompany dinner. You may omit the sugar.

1 cup brown rice flour*
2/3 cup potato starch
1/3 cup tapioca flour
2 teaspoons sugar or 1 teaspoon honey
2 teaspoons xanthan gum
3/4 teaspoon salt
1/2 teaspoon cream of tartar

1/2 teaspoon baking soda
1 large egg, lightly beaten
1 1/3 cups non-fat plain yogurt**
2 tablespoons canola, safflower, or other oil
1 tablespoon caraway seeds
cooking spray

Coat two 5 x 2 1/2-inch nonstick pans (or 8 x 4-inch nonstick pan) with cooking spray. This bread can also be baked in a 7-inch round casserole, but it slices better for sandwiches in the rectangular pans. Preheat oven to 375 degrees.

Combine dry ingredients in large mixing bowl and mix well. With electric mixer on low, add remaining ingredients and blend on medium speed for 2 minutes.

Spoon into prepared pans, smooth tops with wet spatula (if necessary), and bake small pans for 45-50 minutes, large pan for 50-55 minutes or until top is deeply browned and loaf sounds hollow when tapped. Cool on wire rack. Slice with serrated knife or electric knife when bread reaches room temperature.

Preparation = 1 1/4 hours. Serves 8.

Per slice:

								Exchanges		
Calories	Fat	% Fat Cal	Protein	Carbohydrate	Cholesterol	Sodium	Fiber	Carbohydrate	Meat	Fat
215	5 g	19 %	5 g	40 g	23 mg	318 mg	1 g	2 3/4		1

*Flour Alternative: 1 cup bean flour (from Authentic Foods) in place of 1 cup brown rice flour

**Dairy Alternative: 1 cup milk (rice, soy, or nut) in place of 1 1/3 cups yogurt

Irish Soda Bread Without Eggs: Omit egg. Add 2 teaspoons Ener-G Egg Replacer and 1/4 cup water. Bake as directed.

CORN BREAD

(can be made without wheat, gluten, dairy, or refined sugar - see page 9 about ingredients)

I like to serve Corn Bread with Mexican or Southwestern meals, but it goes well with many entrees. This recipe is easy to assemble and very forgiving. Omit the sugar, if you wish.

1/4 cup bean flour* (from Authentic Foods)
3 tablespoons tapioca flour
3 tablespoons potato starch
1/2 teaspoon xanthan gum
1/2 cup yellow or white cornmeal
2 tablespoons sugar or 2 teaspoons honey
1 teaspoon baking powder
1/2 teaspoon baking soda

1/2 teaspoon salt
1 large egg, lightly beaten
2/3 cup buttermilk or 2 teaspoons cider vinegar or Ener-G yeast-free/gluten-free vinegar (reconstituted) plus enough milk (cow, rice, soy or nut) to make 2/3 cup
2 tablespoons canola, safflower or other oil
cooking spray

Coat 8 x 4-inch or 8-inch round or square nonstick pan with cooking spray. Set aside. Preheat oven to 350 degrees.

In medium bowl, combine flours, xanthan gum, cornmeal, sugar (or honey), baking powder, baking soda, and salt. Make a well in center. Set aside.

In another bowl, beat egg, buttermilk, and oil until well blended. Add egg mixture all at once to dry mixture, stirring just until moistened. Batter will be consistency of thick cake batter.

Bake for 20-25 minutes, or until top is firm and edges are lightly browned. Serve warm. (You may also bake the corn bread in 6-muffin tins for 20-25 minutes.)

Preparation = 45 minutes. Serves 6.

Calories	Fat	% Fat Cal	Protein	Carbohydrate	Cholesterol	Sodium	Fiber	Exchanges Carbohydrate	Meat	Fat
180	7 g	33 %	5 g	25 g	32 mg	250 mg	1 g	2		1 1/2

*Flour Alternative: 1/4 cup brown rice flour in place of 1/4 cup bean flour

Corn Bread Without Eggs: Omit egg, add 2 teaspoons Ener-G Egg Replacer and increase buttermilk to 1 cup. Bake for 25-30 minutes or until top is firm and lightly browned.

SPOON BREAD

(can be made without wheat, gluten, dairy, or refined sugar - see page 9 about ingredients)

There are many different versions of spoon bread. Try this one, but feel free to experiment on your own since the dough is very forgiving. Use the green chiles if you like a Southwestern touch. You may omit the cheddar cheese for a dairy-free version.

2 large eggs
1 cup plain yogurt*
1/2 cup finely chopped onion
2 tablespoons canola, safflower, or other oil
4 ounces diced green chiles (1 can) (optional)
1 teaspoon baking powder

1 teaspoon garlic salt
3/4 cup yellow cornmeal
1 cup corn kernels
1 cup shredded low-fat cheddar cheese (cow or soy)
cooking spray

Spray a 9-inch cast iron skillet or 9-inch round or square baking pan with cooking spray. Preheat oven to 350 degrees.

In a large bowl, beat eggs with wire whisk. Add yogurt, onion, oil, and chiles (if using) and mix well.

In another bowl, combine baking powder, garlic salt, and cornmeal. Add to egg mixture. Stir in the corn and 1/2 cup of the cheddar cheese. (If using soy cheddar cheese, add all cheese to batter since it won't melt on top.) Batter will be soft.

Pour batter into prepared pans. Sprinkle remaining 1/2 cup of (cow) cheese over top. Bake for 40-50 minutes, or until top is golden brown. Spoon out of pan.

Preparation = 1 hour. Serves 8.

Calories	Fat	% Fat Cal	Protein	Carbohydrate	Cholesterol	Sodium	Fiber	Exchanges Carbohydrate	Meat	Fat
170	6 g	33 %	8 g	18 g	49 mg	208 mg	2 g	1 1/4		1 1/2

*Dairy Alternative: 3/4 cup milk (rice, soy, or nut) in place of yogurt

ZUCCHINI BREAD

(can be made without wheat, gluten, dairy, or refined sugar - see page 9 about ingredients)

If your garden produced a bumper crop of zucchini this year—or your neighbor just gave you bushels of zucchini—then this recipe is the answer. Bake several batches and freeze for later use.

3 tablespoons canola, safflower, or other oil
2/3 cup brown sugar, packed*
2 large eggs
1 teaspoon gluten-free vanilla extract
1/2 cup applesauce or apple butter
1 cup brown rice flour
1/2 cup potato starch
1/4 cup tapioca flour
2 teaspoons baking powder
1/2 teaspoon xanthan gum
1/2 teaspoon salt
1 1/2 teaspoons ground cinnamon
1 1/2 cups finely grated zucchini (about 3 small zucchini)
1/2 cup chopped pecans (optional)
1/4 cup dark raisins (optional - avoid if sensitive to yeast and mold)

Preheat oven to 350 degrees. Coat 9 x 5-inch nonstick pan with cooking spray. (Or, for smaller loaves, use 3 small nonstick loaf pans, approximately 5 x 2 1/2-inches each.)

In large bowl, cream the oil and sugar (or dried cane juice or honey) together with electric mixer. Add eggs, vanilla, and applesauce and beat well. Add the flours, baking powder, xanthan gum, salt, and cinnamon. Mix thoroughly on medium speed until thoroughly combined. Quickly (but gently) stir in zucchini (and nuts and raisins, if using). Batter will be thick. Turn batter into prepared pans.

Bake 9 x 5-inch loaf for 1 hour; 5 x 2 1/2-inch pans for 45 minutes. Cool on wire rack before cutting.

Preparation = Up to 1 1/4 hours. Serves 8.

Calories	Fat	% Fat Cal	Protein	Carbohydrate	Cholesterol	Sodium	Fiber	Exchanges Carbohydrate	Meat	Fat
300	9 g	27 %	4 g	53 g	45 mg	246 mg	2 g	3 1/2		2

*Sugar Alternative #1: 2/3 cup dried cane juice or maple sugar in place of 2/3 cup brown sugar. Add 1/4 teaspoon baking soda.

*Sugar Alternative #2: 1/3 cup honey in place of 2/3 cup brown sugar. Add 1/4 teaspoon baking soda.

ZUCCHINI BREAD WITHOUT EGGS

(can be made without wheat, gluten, dairy, eggs, or refined sugar - see page 9 about ingredients)

The bean flour in this recipe provides an excellent texture, even though there are no eggs. The breads freeze well, too. For best results, cool to room temperature before slicing with serrated knife or electric knife.

3 tablespoons canola, safflower, or other oil
1/3 cup honey or maple syrup
1/3 cup milk (cow, rice, soy, or nut)
1 teaspoon gluten-free vanilla extract
1 teaspoon molasses
1/2 cup bean flour* (from Authentic Foods)
1/2 cup brown rice flour
1/2 cup potato starch
1/4 cup tapioca flour
2 1/2 teaspoons baking powder
1/2 teaspoon xanthan gum

3/4 teaspoon salt
1/4 teaspoon soy lecithin granules (optional)
1 1/4 teaspoons ground cinnamon
1/8 teaspoon ground cardamom (optional)
1/8 teaspoon ground mace (optional)
1 1/2 cups finely grated zucchini (about
    3 small zucchini or 2 medium)
1/2 cup dark raisins or currants (optional) -
    avoid if sensitive to yeast or mold
1/2 cup chopped pecans or walnuts (optional)
cooking spray

Preheat oven to 350 degrees. Spray three 5 x 2 1/2-inch nonstick pans or a 9 x 5-inch nonstick pan with cooking spray. (Bread bakes more thoroughly in smaller pans.)

Combine oil, honey, milk, vanilla, and molasses in measuring cup and set aside.

In large mixing bowl, combine flours, baking powder, xanthan gum, salt, lecithin, and spices. Add liquid ingredients and mix with electric mixer until thoroughly blended. Stir in zucchini (and raisins and pecans, if using). Batter will be like soft cookie dough.

Spoon batter into prepared pans and smooth tops with spatula. Bake small pans for 35-40 minutes; large pan for 45 minutes to 1 hour.

Preparation = 1 hour to 1 1/4 hours. Serves 8.

| | | | | | | | | Exchanges | | |
Calories	Fat	% Fat Cal	Protein	Carbohydrate	Cholesterol	Sodium	Fiber	Carbohydrate	Meat	Fat
290	9 g	27 %	4 g	51 g	1 mg	217 mg	3 g	3 1/2		2

NOTE: If raisins and nuts are omitted, use two instead of three 5 x 2 1/2-inch pans because the volume of the bread is considerably reduced.

*Flour Alternative: 1/2 cup brown rice flour instead of 1/2 cup bean flour. However, the texture will be better with bean flour.

YEAST-FREE BREADSTICKS WITHOUT EGGS

(can be made without wheat, gluten, dairy, eggs, or refined sugar - see page 9 about ingredients)

Breadsticks are fun to eat and make a nice complement to any meal, especially Italian meals. But they don't have to contain yeast. This flavorful version is fast and easy.

3/4 cup brown rice flour*
1/4 cup sweet rice flour
2 tablespoons tapioca flour
1 teaspoon xanthan gum
1 teaspoon sugar or 1/2 teaspoon honey
1 1/2 teaspoons baking powder
1/2 teaspoon salt
1/2 teaspoon onion powder

1/4 teaspoon Italian herb seasoning
3/4 cup milk (cow, rice, soy, or nut)
cooking spray

TOPPING
1/4 teaspoon salt
1 teaspoon Italian herb seasoning
2 teaspoons sesame seeds (optional)

Preheat oven to 425 degrees. Coat a large baking sheet with cooking spray and set aside.

In food processor, combine flours, xanthan gum, sugar (or honey), baking powder, salt, onion powder, Italian herb seasoning and milk. Blend thoroughly. Dough will be soft.

Place dough in large, *heavy-duty* plastic freezer bag that has 1/2-inch opening cut diagonally on one corner. (This makes a 1-inch diameter opening.) Squeeze dough out of plastic bag onto cookie sheet in 10 strips, each 1-inch wide by 6 inches long. Hold the bag of dough upright as you squeeze, rather than at an angle. Spray breadsticks with cooking spray. Sprinkle with salt, Italian herb seasoning, and sesame seeds (if using).

Bake at 425 degrees for 15-20 minutes or until browned to desired degree. Switch position of cookie sheet halfway through baking to assure even browning. Cool on wire rack. When cool, store in airtight container. Makes 10.

Preparation Time = 40 minutes. Serves 10 (1 breadstick each).

Per breadstick ... Exchanges

Calories	Fat	% Fat Cal	Protein	Carbohydrate	Cholesterol	Sodium	Fiber	Carbohydrate	Meat	Fat
80	1 g	14 %	2 g	16 g	2 mg	225 mg	1 g	1		1/4

*Flour Alternative: 3/4 cup bean flour (from Authentic Foods) in place of 3/4 cup brown rice flour

NOTE: If using electric mixer instead of food processor, add 2 tablespoons water so batter is consistency of soft cookie dough.

YEAST-FREE PIZZA CRUST

(can be made without wheat, gluten, dairy, eggs, or refined sugar - see page 9 about ingredients)

This recipe proves you can have your favorite pizza, even if you have food sensitivities. Top with your favorite sauce and toppings. You may omit the sugar, if you wish.

1/2 cup brown rice flour or bean flour
  (from Authentic Foods)
1/2 cup tapioca flour
1 teaspoon sugar or 1/2 teaspoon honey
1 teaspoon xanthan gum
1/2 teaspoon salt
1/4 teaspoon unflavored gelatin powder
1/2 teaspoon baking powder
1/2 teaspoon baking soda
1/2 teaspoon onion powder

1/2 teaspoon crushed rosemary leaves
1/2 teaspoon Italian herb seasoning
1 large egg or 1 teaspoon Ener-G Egg
  Replacer powder dissolved in 3 tablespoons water
1/2 cup milk (cow, rice, soy, or nut)
1 tablespoon olive oil
cooking spray
(Use Pizza Sauce of your choice or see
  page 134 for a flavorful version.)

Preheat oven to 400 degrees. Spray pan with cooking spray, using a 13 x 9-inch nonstick baking sheet or 12-inch nonstick pizza pan for a thin, crispy crust or a 11 x 7-inch nonstick pan or a 10-inch cast-iron skillet for a deep-dish crust.

In small mixing bowl, combine all ingredients. Mix with electric mixer (using regular beaters) for 2 minutes. Batter will be like soft cookie dough and very sticky.

Spread batter in prepared pan, using a wet spatula to smooth the dough and push it up to—but not touching—the outer edges of pan. Make a little ridge around the edge to contain the pizza sauce and toppings.

Bake for 15 minutes. Remove from oven, top with toppings, and bake another 10-15 minutes or until browned to taste. If using eggs, the batter will rise and fall during baking.

Preparation = 40 minutes. Serves 6.

Pizza Crust Only:

Calories	Fat	% Fat Cal	Protein	Carbohydrate	Cholesterol	Sodium	Fiber	Exchanges Carbohydrate	Meat	Fat
162	4 g	22 %	3 g	30 g	33 mg	334 mg	<1 g	2		3/4

YEAST-FREE FOCACCIA

(can be made without wheat, gluten, dairy, or refined sugar - see page 9 about ingredients)

Focaccia is such a popular bread these days. Now you can enjoy this Italian bread (which is a cross between pizza and flatbread) without the ingredients you can't have. Pan size determines shape and thickness of the bread. You may omit the sugar, if you wish.

1 cup brown or white rice flour
2/3 cup potato starch
1/3 cup tapioca flour
2 teaspoons sugar or 1/2 teaspoon honey
2 teaspoons xanthan gum
3/4 teaspoon salt
1/2 teaspoon unflavored gelatin powder
1 teaspoon baking powder
1 1/4 teaspoons baking soda
3/4 teaspoon onion powder
1 teaspoon crushed rosemary leaves

2 large eggs
1 cup milk (cow, rice, soy, or nut)
2 tablespoons olive oil
cooking spray

TOPPING
1 1/2 teaspoons Italian herb seasoning
1/2 teaspoon salt
1 tablespoon olive oil (or you may use cooking spray)
1/4 cup Parmesan cheese (cow, rice, or soy)

Preheat oven to 375 degrees. Coat 11 x 7-inch, two 8-inch round, or a 13 x 9-inch nonstick baking pan with cooking spray. (Use the 11 x 7-inch pan or 8-inch pans for thicker bread that can be sliced horizontally for sandwiches. Use the 13 x 9-inch pan for thinner bread that can serve as a pizza crust.)

Combine dry ingredients in large mixing bowl. With electric mixer on low, add eggs, milk, and oil to bowl and blend on medium speed for 2 minutes. Dough will be soft and sticky. Use spatula dipped in cold water to spread batter in pan. Sprinkle or spray with olive oil and sprinkle with Italian herb seasoning and salt.

Bake for 20-25 minutes or until top is well browned. Dust with Parmesan cheese.

Preparation = 45 minutes. Serves 8.

| | | | | | | | | Exchanges | | |
Calories	Fat	% Fat Cal	Protein	Carbohydrate	Cholesterol	Sodium	Fiber	Carbohydrate	Meat	Fat
255	9 g	29 %	5 g	41 g	51 mg	654 mg	1 g	3		2

Serving Suggestions: Cut into squares approximately 3 x 3 inches, or slice the entire round loaf horizontally, place sandwich fillings on bottom half and replace top half. Slice into wedges and serve. Or use the Focaccia as a yeast-free pizza crust with your favorite toppings. (See page 42.)

Variations: For additional toppings, see Focaccia Toppings on page 23.

YEAST-FREE FOCACCIA WITHOUT EGGS #1

(can be made without wheat, gluten, dairy, eggs, or refined sugar - see page 9 about ingredients)

I developed this recipe for my students who have serious, multiple allergies so they, too, could enjoy this wonderful Italian flatbread. Pan size determines shape and thickness of bread.

1 cup brown or white rice flour
2/3 cup potato starch
1/3 cup tapioca flour
2 teaspoons sugar or 1/2 teaspoon honey
2 teaspoons xanthan gum
3/4 teaspoon salt
1/2 teaspoon unflavored gelatin powder
1 teaspoon baking powder
1 1/4 teaspoons baking soda
3/4 teaspoon onion powder
1 teaspoon crushed rosemary leaves

2 teaspoons Ener-G Egg Replacer powder dissolved in 1/4 cup water)
1 cup milk (cow, rice, soy, or nut)
2 tablespoons olive oil

TOPPING
1 1/2 teaspoons Italian herb seasoning
1/2 teaspoon salt
1 tablespoon olive oil (or you may use cooking spray of choice)
1/4 cup Parmesan cheese (cow, rice, or soy - optional)

Preheat oven to 375 degrees. Coat 11 x 7-inch, two 8-inch, or a 13 x 9-inch nonstick baking pan with cooking spray. (Use the 11 x 7-inch pan or 8-inch pans for thicker bread that can be sliced horizontally for sandwiches. Use the 13 x 9-inch pan for thinner bread that can serve as a pizza crust.)

Combine dry ingredients in large mixing bowl. With electric mixer on low, add eggs (or Egg Replacer mixed in water), milk, and oil to bowl and blend on medium speed for 2 minutes. Spoon into pan. Sprinkle or spray with olive oil and sprinkle with Italian herb seasoning and salt. Bake for 15-20 minutes or until top is lightly browned. Dust with Parmesan cheese.

Preparation = 45 minutes. Serves 8.

| | | | | | | | | Exchanges | | |
Calories	Fat	% Fat Cal	Protein	Carbohydrate	Cholesterol	Sodium	Fiber	Carbohydrate	Meat	Fat
210	7 g	3 2 %	5 g	31 g	6 mg	641 mg	1 g	2		1 1/2

Serving Suggestions: Cut into squares approximately 3 x 3 inches. Or slice the entire round loaf horizontally, place sandwich fillings on bottom half and replace top half. Slice into wedges and serve. Or use the Focaccia as a yeast-free pizza crust with your favorite toppings. (See page 42.)

Variations: For additional toppings, see Focaccia Toppings on page 23.

YEAST-FREE FOCACCIA WITHOUT EGGS #2

(can be made without wheat, gluten, dairy, eggs, or refined sugar - see page 9 about ingredients)

Don't be surprised by the tofu in this recipe. It replaces the eggs in this flavorful Italian flatbread, producing a moist herb bread. Pan size determines shape and thickness of bread. You may omit the sugar, if you wish.

1 cup boiling water
1/2 cup soft silken tofu by Mori-Nu®
1 cup brown or white rice flour
2/3 cup potato starch
1/3 cup tapioca flour
2 teaspoons sugar or 1/2 teaspoon honey
2 teaspoons xanthan gum
3/4 teaspoon salt
1/2 teaspoon unflavored gelatin powder
1 1/4 teaspoons baking soda
3/4 teaspoon onion powder

1 teaspoon crushed rosemary leaves
3 tablespoons canola, safflower, or other oil

TOPPING
1 tablespoon olive oil (or you may use cooking spray)
1 1/2 teaspoons Italian herb seasoning
1/2 teaspoon salt
1/4 cup Parmesan cheese (cow, rice, or soy - optional)

Preheat oven to 375 degrees. Coat two 8 x 8-inch round or square nonstick pans (or a 11 x 7-inch or 13 x 9-inch pan) with cooking spray. Set aside.

In food processor, blend together the hot water and tofu until very smooth. Add remaining ingredients and blend until smooth. Dough will be very, very soft.

Spoon into prepared pan(s) and smooth top with knife (if necessary). Sprinkle or spray with olive oil, then sprinkle with Italian herb seasoning, salt, and Parmesan cheese. Bake for 15-20 minutes for 11 x 7-inch pans or 25 minutes for 8-inch pans or 15-20 minutes for 13 x 9-inch pans—or until tops are firm.

Cool pan on wire rack for 5 minutes before slicing.

Preparation = 30 minutes. Serves 8.

| | | | | | | | | Exchanges | | |
Calories	Fat	% Fat Cal	Protein	Carbohydrate	Cholesterol	Sodium	Fiber	Carbohydrate	Meat	Fat
240	9 g	34 %	3 g	37 g	2 mg	627 mg	1 g	2 1/2		2

Variations: For additional toppings, see Focaccia Toppings on page 23.

BREAKFAST BREADS & DISHES

Eat your breakfast.— Everybody's mother

Breakfast is the meal that can be most frustrating for those on special diets. For some of us, it's just not breakfast without muffins, bagels, waffles, or pancakes. Enjoy!

Yeast-Free Breakfast Breads and Dishes

Breakfast Yeast Breads

See page 9 for information on the special ingredients used in these recipes.

BAKED DOUGHNUTS

(can be made without wheat, gluten, dairy, or refined sugar - see page 9 about ingredients)

These doughnuts are flavorful, yet low-fat because they are baked rather than fried.

1 cup brown rice
1/2 cup potato starch
1/2 cup tapioca flour
2 teaspoons xanthan gum
1 teaspoon unflavored gelatin powder
1 1/2 teaspoons baking powder
1 1/2 teaspoons baking soda
1/2 teaspoon salt
2 teaspoons ground cinnamon
1/4 teaspoon ground cloves
1/4 teaspoon ground nutmeg
1 large egg, lightly beaten

2/3 cup brown sugar, firmly packed*
1/2 cup apple juice frozen concentrate
1/2 cup applesauce or prune baby food
1/2 cup pure maple syrup or honey
3 tablespoons canola, safflower, or other oil
cooking spray

FROSTING (optional)
1 1/4 cups powdered sugar
1 teaspoon vanilla extract
1/4 cup pure maple syrup

Preheat oven to 375 degrees. Coat molds of mini-Bundt or mini-angel food cake pans with cooking spray. (Or use 6-muffin or cupcake tins.)

In small mixing bowl, stir together the flours, xanthan gum, gelatin powder, baking powder, baking soda, salt, cinnamon, cloves, and nutmeg. Set aside.

In another bowl, combine the egg, brown sugar, apple juice concentrate (thawed) and applesauce (or prunes), maple syrup, and oil. Stir in dry ingredients until just moistened.

Divide the batter in half since you'll be baking the batter in two batches (unless you have two baking pans). Spoon half of the batter into prepared mini-molds—about 2 generous tablespoons per mold. (If using muffin tins, fill each two-thirds full.)

Bake for 20-25 minutes or until tops spring back when touched lightly. Loosen edges of doughnuts and turn out into a rack to cool. Clean pan, spray again with cooking spray, and fill molds with 2 tablespoons of batter each. Bake for 20-25 minutes.

To frost, combine powdered sugar, vanilla, and maple syrup, adding more maple syrup, if needed, to make frosting of spreading consistency. Dip the rounded side of doughnut into frosting and set on waxed paper until frosting is firm. Makes 12.

Preparation = 45 minutes. Serves 12.

Per doughnut without frosting:

Calories	Fat	% Fat Cal	Protein	Carbohydrate	Cholesterol	Sodium	Fiber	Exchanges Carbohydrate	Meat	Fat
230	4 g	16 %	2 g	47 g	15 mg	307 mg	1 g	3		1

Per doughnut with frosting:

Calories	Fat	% Fat Cal	Protein	Carbohydrate	Cholesterol	Sodium	Fiber	Exchanges Carbohydrate	Meat	Fat
295	4 g	13 %	2 g	64 g	15 mg	307 mg	1 g	4 1/4		1

*Sugar Alternative: 2/3 cup dried cane juice or maple sugar in place of brown sugar. Increase baking soda to 1 3/4 teaspoons.

BAKED DOUGHNUTS WITHOUT EGGS

(can be made without wheat, gluten, dairy, eggs, or refined sugar - see page 9 about ingredients)

Fruit puree and tofu bind the ingredients in place of eggs in these fragrant, flavorful doughnuts.

1/4 cup soft silken tofu by Mori-Nu®
1/2 cup apple juice frozen concentrate
1/2 cup pure maple syrup
1/2 cup applesauce or apple butter
2/3 cup brown sugar, firmly packed*
3 tablespoons canola, safflower, or other oil
1 cup brown rice flour
1/2 cup potato starch
1/2 cup tapioca flour
2 teaspoons xanthan gum
1 teaspoon unflavored gelatin powder
1 1/2 teaspoons baking powder

1 1/2 teaspoons baking soda
1/2 teaspoon salt
2 teaspoons ground cinnamon
1/4 teaspoon ground cloves
1/4 teaspoon ground nutmeg
cooking spray

FROSTING (optional)
4 ounces extra-firm silken tofu (1/2 cup)
   by Mori-Nu®
1/3 to 1/2 cup honey
1 teaspoon gluten-free vanilla extract

Preheat oven to 375 degrees. Coat molds of a mini-Bundt or mini-angel food cake pans with cooking spray. (Or use 6-muffin or cupcake tins.)

In food processor, puree the tofu, apple juice concentrate (thawed), maple syrup, applesauce (or apple butter), brown sugar, and oil until mixture is very, very smooth—about 3 minutes. In a large mixing bowl, stir together the flours, xanthan gum, gelatin powder, baking powder, baking soda, salt, cinnamon, cloves, and nutmeg. Add tofu mixture to dry ingredients and stir just until moistened. Batter will be very soft.

Divide the batter in half since you'll be baking the batter in two batches (unless you have two baking pans). Spoon half of the batter into prepared mini-molds—about 2 generous tablespoons per mold. (If using muffin tins, fill two-thirds full.)

Bake for 20-25 minutes or until tops spring back when touched lightly. Loosen edges of doughnuts and turn out onto a rack to cool. Clean pan, spray again with cooking spray and fill molds with 2 tablespoons of batter each. Bake for 20-25 minutes.

To frost, combine tofu, honey, and vanilla in food processor and blend until very, very smooth. Dip rounded side of doughnut into frosting. Makes 12.

Preparation = 45 minutes. Serves 12.

Per doughnut without frosting:

Calories	Fat	% Fat Cal	Protein	Carbohydrate	Cholesterol	Sodium	Fiber	Exchanges Carbohydrate	Meat	Fat
200	4 g	18%	1 g	42 g	0 mg	301 mg	1 g	3		1

Per doughnut with frosting:

Calories	Fat	% Fat Cal	Protein	Carbohydrate	Cholesterol	Sodium	Fiber	Exchanges Carbohydrate	Meat	Fat
275	4 g	14%	2 g	59 g	0 mg	310 mg	1 g	4		1

*Sugar Alternative: 2/3 cup dried cane juice or maple sugar in place of 2/3 cup brown sugar. Increase baking soda to 1 3/4 teaspoons.

BANANA BREAD

(can be made without wheat, gluten, dairy, or refined sugar - see page 9 about ingredients))

Don't throw away those extra-ripe bananas! The high sugar level and fuller flavor of these bananas makes them perfect for banana bread. If the bananas ripen before you're ready to bake bread, just freeze the mashed pulp until you're ready to bake. Defrost before using.

3 tablespoons canola, safflower, or other oil
2/3 cup brown sugar, packed*
2 large eggs
1 teaspoon gluten-free vanilla extract
1 cup brown rice flour or bean flour (from Authentic Foods)
1/2 cup potato starch
1/4 cup tapioca flour
1/2 teaspoon xanthan gum
1/2 teaspoon salt

2 teaspoons baking powder
1 teaspoon ground cinnamon
1/8 teaspoon ground cardamom (optional)
1/8 teaspoon ground mace (optional)
1 1/2 cups mashed ripe bananas
1/2 cup chopped pecans or walnuts (optional)
1/2 cup raisins (optional - avoid if sensitive to yeast or mold)
cooking spray

Preheat oven to 350 degrees. Coat 9 x 5-inch nonstick pan with cooking spray. (Or, for smaller loaves which will bake more thoroughly, use 3 small loaf pans, approximately 5 x 2 1/2-inches each.)

Cream the oil, sugar, eggs, and vanilla together. Mix together the flours, xanthan gum, salt, baking powder, and spices. Add flour mixture to egg mixture, alternating with bananas. Stir in nuts. Batter will be somewhat soft.

Bake 9 x 5-inch loaf for 1 hour; 5 x 2 1/2-inch pans for 45 minutes. Cool on wire rack before cutting.

Preparation = Up to 1 1/4 hours. Serves 8.

| | | | | | | | | Exchanges | | |
Calories	Fat	% Fat Cal	Protein	Carbohydrate	Cholesterol	Sodium	Fiber	Carbohydrate	Meat	Fat
285	9 g	25 %	3 g	51 g	45 mg	245 mg	2 g	3 1/2		2

*Sugar Alternative #1: 2/3 cup dried cane juice or maple sugar in place of 2/3 cup brown sugar. Add 1/4 teaspoon baking soda.

*Sugar Alternative #2: 1/3 cup pure maple syrup in place of 2/3 cup brown sugar. Add 1/4 teaspoon baking soda.

BANANA BREAD WITHOUT EGGS

(can be made without wheat, gluten, dairy, eggs, or refined sugar - see page 9 about ingredients)

Banana bread works especially well without eggs because the bananas help to bind the ingredients together. For best results, let bread cool to room temperature before slicing.

1   cup mashed ripe bananas (about 3 small)
3   tablespoons canola, safflower, or other oil
1/3   cup honey or pure maple syrup
1/3   cup milk (cow, rice, soy, or nut)
1   teaspoon gluten-free vanilla extract
1   teaspoon molasses
1/2   cup brown rice flour
1/2   cup bean flour (from Authentic Foods)
3/4   cup potato starch
2 1/2   teaspoons baking powder

1/2   teaspoon xanthan gum
1/2   teaspoon salt
1/4   teaspoon soy lecithin granules
1 1/4   teaspoons ground cinnamon
1/8   teaspoon ground cardamom (optional)
1/8   teaspoon ground mace (optional)
1/2   cup dark raisins or currants (optional
   avoid if sensitive to yeast or mold)
1/2   cup chopped pecans or walnuts (option
cooking spray

Preheat oven to 350 degrees. Spray three 5 x 2 1/2-inch nonstick pans or a 9 x 5-inch nonstick pan with cooking spray. (Bread will bake more thoroughly in smaller pans.)

In large mixing bowl with electric mixer, cream together the mashed bananas, oil, honey, milk, vanilla, and molasses until thoroughly blended. Add flours, baking powder, xanthan gum, salt, lecithin, and spices and mix together thoroughly. Stir in raisins and nuts, if using. Batter will be somewhat soft. Spoon batter into prepared pan(s) and smooth batter with spatula.

Bake small pans for 35-40 minutes; large pan for 50-60 minutes or until tops are golden brown. Cool on wire rack. Slice with serrated knife or electric knife.

Preparation = 1 hour to 1 1/4 hours. Serves 8.

| | | | | | | | | Exchanges | | |
Calories	Fat	% Fat Cal	Protein	Carbohydrate	Cholesterol	Sodium	Fiber	Carbohydrate	Meat	Fat
300	9 g	26 %	4 g	53 g	53 mg	263 mg	3 g	3 1/2		2

NOTE: If raisins and nuts are omitted, use two instead of three 5 x 2 1/2-inch pans because the volume of the bread is considerably reduced. Banana bread without nuts and raisins may be somewhat gummier, but baking in smaller pans will help reduce this problem.

BLUEBERRY MUFFINS

(can be made without wheat, gluten, dairy, or refined sugar - see page 9 about ingredients)

For best results, bake these muffins in the 12-muffin size rather than 6-muffin tins. Freeze blueberries in the summer when they're plentiful. Then toss them into the batter (frozen) just before spooning into muffin tins to avoid "blue" batter. Increase baking time by 5 minutes.

1 cup brown rice flour*
1/2 cup potato starch
1/2 cup tapioca flour
1 teaspoon unflavored gelatin powder
1 teaspoon xanthan gum
2 1/2 teaspoons baking powder
1/3 cup sugar or 3 tablespoons honey
3/4 teaspoon salt
3/4 cup milk (cow, rice, soy, or nut)
1/4 cup canola, safflower, or other oil

2 large eggs, lightly beaten
1 teaspoon gluten-free vanilla extract
2 teaspoons grated lemon peel
1 1/4 cups blueberries, fresh or frozen
cooking spray or paper muffin liners

GLAZE
2 tablespoons powdered sugar or
  1 tablespoon honey
2 tablespoons lemon juice

Preheat oven to 400 degrees. Coat a 12-cup muffin tin (2-inch diameter base, 1 1/4-inch deep) with cooking spray or use paper muffin liners.

Stir together the flours, gelatin powder, xanthan gum, baking powder, sugar (if using honey, add with liquid ingredients), and salt in large bowl. Make well in center.

In a small bowl, combine milk, oil, eggs, vanilla extract, and lemon peel. Pour into well of flour mixture. Stir just until ingredients are moistened. Gently fold in blueberries. Batter will be very soft. Spoon batter into muffin tins.

Bake for approximately 25 minutes, or until tops of muffins are lightly browned. Remove from oven. Combine powdered sugar (or honey) and lemon juice to form glaze. Drizzle over warm muffins. Makes 12.

Preparation = 40 minutes. Serves 12.

Per Muffin:

Calories	Fat	% Fat Cal	Protein	Carbohydrate	Cholesterol	Sodium	Fiber	Exchanges Carbohydrate	Meat	Fat
210	6 g	26 %	3 g	37 g	32 mg	229 mg	1 g	2 1/2		1 1/4

*Flour Alternative: 1 cup bean flour (from Authentic Foods) in place of 1 cup brown rice flour

Cranberry-Orange Muffins: Substitute 1 cup chopped frozen cranberries or 1/2 cup dried cranberries for the blueberries. Replace grated lemon peel with 1 tablespoon of grated orange peel. (Muffins will be smaller due to loss of volume from blueberries.)

BLUEBERRY MUFFINS WITHOUT EGGS

(can be made without wheat, gluten, dairy, eggs, or refined sugar - see page 9 about ingredients)

If you love Blueberry Muffins but can't eat eggs—this is the recipe for you. These muffins will be somewhat heavier than the muffins on the previous page, but they'll taste fabulous! They're best warm from the oven. If any are left over, store in airtight container.

1 1/4 cups brown or white rice flour*
3/4 cup potato starch
1/2 cup tapioca flour
1 teaspoon unflavored gelatin powder
1 teaspoon xanthan gum
1 1/4 teaspoons baking powder
1 1/4 teaspoons baking soda
1 teaspoon salt
1/2 cup sugar**
1 1/4 cups milk (cow, rice, soy, or nut)

1/4 cup canola, safflower, or other oil
1 teaspoon gluten-free vanilla extract
grated lemon peel of 1 lemon (1 tablespoon)
1 1/4 cups blueberries, fresh or frozen
cooking spray or paper muffin liners

GLAZE (optional)
1 tablespoon honey
2 tablespoons lemon juice

Preheat oven to 375 degrees. Coat a 12-cup muffin tin (2-inch diameter base, 1 1/4-inch deep) with cooking spray or use paper muffin liners. In large mixing bowl, combine flours, gelatin, xanthan gum, baking powder, baking soda, salt, and sugar. Make well in center. Set aside.

In medium bowl, whisk together milk, oil, vanilla, and lemon peel. Stir liquid mixture into dry ingredients. Gently fold blueberries into batter, which will be the consistency of thick cake batter. Distribute batter evenly among muffin tins.

Bake for 20-25 minutes or until toothpick inserted in center comes out clean. Remove from oven. While muffins are still warm, brush with mixture of honey and lemon juice. (For best results, warm honey and lemon juice in microwave for easier brushing.)

Preparation = 40 minutes. Serves 12.

Per Muffin:

Calories	Fat	% Fat Cal	Protein	Carbohydrate	Cholesterol	Sodium	Fiber	Exchanges Carbohydrate	Meat	Fat
235	6 g	22 %	2 g	45 g	38 mg	209 mg	1 g	3		1

*Flour Alternative: 1 1/4 cups bean flour (from Authentic Foods) in place of 1 1/4 brown or white rice flour

**Sugar Alternative: 1/3 cup honey in place of 1/2 cup sugar. Reduce milk to 1 cup.

MUFFIN MIX

(can be made without wheat, gluten, dairy, or refined sugar - see page 9 about ingredients)

Store this muffin mix in an airtight container. It makes 4 batches of muffins. For savory dinner or luncheon muffins, reduce the sugar and add your favorite herbs and spices.

4 cups white or brown rice flour
2 cups potato starch
2 cups tapioca flour
4 teaspoons xanthan gum

3 tablespoons + 1 teaspoon baking powder
3 teaspoons salt
4 teaspoons unflavored gelatin powder
1 1/2 cups sugar (cane, unbleached cane, fructose powder, or dried cane juice

For one batch of 12 muffins:

2 cups MUFFIN MIX
1/4 cup canola, safflower, or other oil
2 large eggs, lightly beaten
1 teaspoon gluten-free vanilla extract
3/4 cup milk (cow, rice, soy, or nut)
cooking spray or paper muffin liners

GLAZE (Optional)
2 tablespoons powdered sugar
2 tablespoons lemon juice
    (or simply dust with powdered sugar)

Preheat oven to 400 degrees. Coat a 12-cup muffin tin (2-inch diameter base, 1 1/4-inch deep) with cooking spray or use paper muffin liners. Set aside.

Place MUFFIN MIX in large mixing bowl. Make well in center.

In another bowl, combine oil, eggs, vanilla, milk, (and citrus peel, if using). Pour into well of flour mixture. Stir just until ingredients are moistened. Gently stir in additional ingredients (blueberries, poppy seeds, cranberries, etc.). Spoon dough into muffin tins.

Bake for approximately 25 minutes (30 minutes if using frozen blueberries) or until muffin tops are lightly browned. Remove from oven. Combine powdered sugar and lemon juice to form glaze (if using). Drizzle over warm muffins. Makes 12.

Preparation = 40 minutes. Serves 12.

Lemon Poppy-Seed Muffins: Add 3 tablespoons grated lemon peel and 2 tablespoons poppy seeds. Serves 12.

Per Muffin: Exchanges

Calories	Fat	% Fat Cal	Protein	Carbohydrate	Cholesterol	Sodium	Fiber	Carbohydrate	Meat	Fat
213	7 g	29 %	3 g	36 g	32 mg	228 mg	1 g	2 1/2		1 1/4

Blueberry-Lemon Muffins: Add grated lemon peel from 1 lemon and 1 1/4 cups fresh or frozen blueberries. (See page 53 for nutrient content.)

Cranberry-Orange Muffins: Add 2 teaspoons grated orange peel and 1 cup chopped frozen cranberries. (See page 53 for nutrient content.)

NOTE: Muffins without added nuts or fruit (e.g., blueberries, cranberries, etc.) will have less volume and therefore make smaller muffins.

BRAN MUFFINS

(can be made without wheat, gluten, dairy, or refined sugar - see page 9 about ingredients)

Bran muffins are packed with flavor and the rice polish or rice bran adds important fiber. Their delightful aroma will fill your kitchen as they bake. They freeze well, too.

3/4 cup brown rice flour*
1/2 cup potato starch
1/4 cup tapioca flour
2 tablespoons rice bran or rice polish
1/3 cup brown sugar, packed**
1 teaspoon baking powder
1/2 teaspoon baking soda
1 teaspoon xanthan gum
1/4 teaspoon soy lecithin granules (optional)
1/4 teaspoon ground nutmeg
1 teaspoon cinnamon
1/4 teaspoon ground ginger
1/4 teaspoon allspice

1/2 teaspoon salt
2/3 cup milk (cow, rice, soy, or nut)
1 tablespoon Ener-G yeast-free/gluten-free vinegar (reconstituted) or cider vinegar
1 large egg
2 tablespoons canola, safflower, or other oil
1/3 cup molasses
1 teaspoon gluten-free vanilla
1/2 cup raisins (optional - avoid if sensitive to yeast or mold)
1/4 cup chopped walnuts (optional)
cooking spray or use paper muffin liners

Preheat oven to 375 degrees. Coat a 12-cup muffin tin (2-inch diameter base, 1 1/4-inch deep) with cooking spray or use paper muffin liners.

In large bowl, mix together flours with other dry ingredients. Set aside.

In separate bowl, whisk together milk, vinegar, egg, oil, molasses, and vanilla. Gently stir into dry ingredients just until moistened. Fold in raisins and nuts, if using. Batter will be somewhat soft. Spoon batter into muffin tins.

Bake for 25-30 minutes or until tops are firm. If using 6-muffin tins, increase baking time to 30-40 minutes. Makes 6 large or 12 regular muffins.

Preparation = 40-50 minutes. Serves 12 (regular muffins.)

Per Muffin:								Exchanges		
Calories	Fat	% Fat Cal	Protein	Carbohydrate	Cholesterol	Sodium	Fiber	Carbohydrate	Meat	Fat
180	4 g	20 g	2 g	35 g	17 mg	198 mg	1 g	2 1/4		3/4

*Flour Alternative: 3/4 cup bean flour (from Authentic Foods) in place of 3/4 cup brown rice flour.

**Sugar Alternative #1: 1/3 cup dried cane juice or 1/3 cup date sugar in place of 1/3 cup brown sugar. Increase baking soda to 3/4 teaspoon.

**Sugar Alternative #2: 1/3 cup maple syrup in place of 1/3 cup brown sugar. Reduce milk to 1/2 cup. Increase baking soda to 3/4 teaspoon.

BRAN MUFFINS WITHOUT EGGS

(can be made without wheat, gluten, dairy, eggs, or refined sugar - see page 9 about ingredients)

These muffins are just as flavorful as those without eggs, but they'll be a little more dense.

3/4 cup milk (cow, rice, soy, or nut)
2 tablespoons Ener-G yeast-free/gluten-free vinegar (reconstituted) or cider vinegar
1/4 cup soft silken tofu by Mori-Nu®
2 tablespoons canola, safflower, or other oil
1/3 cup molasses
1 teaspoon gluten-free vanilla
3/4 cup brown rice flour*
1/2 cup potato starch
1/4 cup tapioca flour
2 tablespoons rice bran or rice polish
1/3 cup brown sugar**
1 3/4 teaspoons baking powder

1 teaspoon baking soda
1 teaspoon xanthan gum
1/4 teaspoon ground nutmeg
1 teaspoon cinnamon
1/4 teaspoon ground ginger
1/4 teaspoon allspice
1/8 teaspoon ground cloves
3/4 teaspoon salt
1/2 cup raisins (optional - avoid if sensitive to yeast or mold)
1/4 cup chopped walnuts (optional)
cooking spray or paper muffin liners

Preheat oven to 375 degrees. Coat a 12-cup muffin tin (2-inch diameter base, 1 1/4-inch deep) with cooking spray or paper muffin liners.

In blender, whirl milk, vinegar, and tofu until very, very smooth. Add oil, molasses, and vanilla and blend well. Set aside.

In large bowl, mix together flours with other dry ingredients. Gently stir milk-tofu mixture into dry ingredients just until moistened. Fold in raisins and nuts, if using. Batter will be soft. Spoon batter into muffin tins.

Bake for 25-30 minutes or until tops are firm. If using 6-muffin tins, increase baking time to 30-40 minutes. Makes 6 large or 12 regular muffins.

Preparation = 40-50 minutes. Serves 12 (regular muffins.)

Per Muffin:								Exchanges		
Calories	Fat	% Fat Cal	Protein	Carbohydrate	Cholesterol	Sodium	Fiber	Carbohydrate	Meat	Fat
175	4 g	19 %	2 g	36 g	2 mg	306 mg	1 g	2 1/2		3/4

*Flour Alternative: 3/4 cup bean flour (from Authentic Foods) in place of 3/4 cup brown rice flour.

**Sugar Alternative #1: 1/3 cup dried cane juice or 1/3 cup date sugar in place of brown sugar. Increase baking soda to 1 1/4 teaspoons.

**Sugar Alternative #2: 1/3 cup maple syrup in place of 1/3 cup brown sugar. Reduce milk to 1/2 cup. Increase baking soda to 1 1/4 teaspoons.

BISCUITS

(can be made without wheat, gluten, dairy, eggs, or refined sugar - see page 9 about ingredients)

Biscuits are so versatile—have them for breakfast or use them as buns. Change the ingredients slightly and you have shortbread for fresh strawberries and whipped cream. For best results, push straight down with the biscuit cutter rather than twisting it. The biscuit will rise higher this way. They will also rise slightly higher if you make them as drop biscuits.

1/2 cup white or brown rice flour*
1/4 cup potato starch
1/4 cup tapioca
1 teaspoon granulated sugar or honey
2 teaspoons baking powder
1/2 teaspoon baking soda
1/2 teaspoon xanthan gum
1/4 teaspoon salt (optional)
1 teaspoon Egg Replacer (by Ener-G)

1/4 cup butter or canola oil spread
    (Spectrum™) or vegetable shortening
1/3 cup buttermilk or 1 teaspoon cider
    vinegar or fresh lemon juice or Ener-G
    yeast-free/gluten-free vinegar (reconsti-
    tuted) with enough milk (cow, rice, soy,
    or nut) to equal 1/3 cup
cooking spray

Preheat oven to 425 degrees. Sift the dry ingredients together. Combine butter with dry ingredients using pastry blender or rubbing ingredients together with your fingers.

Add buttermilk and stir until just moistened. Place the mixture on baking sheet that has been coated with cooking spray.

Shape mixture to 1-inch thickness and about 6 x 6-inch square or circle, compressing mixture as little as possible. Cut into 8 round biscuit shapes using 2-inch biscuit cutter or open end of drinking glass. Remove uncut portions of biscuit dough and gently press these portions into 2-inch circles. Or, for easier handling, simply cut dough into 8 square pieces and spread pieces across baking sheet so sides are not touching. Or simply drop biscuits by tablespoonfuls onto sheet. Bake for 10-12 minutes or until lightly browned. Makes 8 biscuits, each 2 inches.

Shortbread: Add 1/4 cup granulated sugar or fructose powder and bake as directed.

Preparation = 30 minutes. Serves 8 (1 biscuit each).

Calories	Fat	% Fat Cal	Protein	Carbohydrate	Cholesterol	Sodium	Fiber	Exchanges Carbohydrate	Meat	Fat
130	6 g	42 %	1 g	18 g	16 mg	328 mg	<1 g	1 1/4		1 1/4

(Using Spectrum™ subtracts 16 cholesterol grams. Shortbread adds 25 calories and 6 carbohydrate grams.)

*Flour Alternative: 1/2 cup bean flour (from Authentic Foods) in place of rice flour

COFFEE CAKE

(can be made without wheat, gluten, dairy, or refined sugar - see page 9 about ingredients)

This produces a moist, fragrant coffee cake that's wonderful plain—or dressed up with cranberries or blueberries. See below.

1/4 cup canola, safflower, or other oil
3/4 cup granulated sugar*
2 large eggs (or 2 egg whites)
1 tablespoon grated orange or lemon peel
1 cup white or brown rice flour
6 tablespoons potato starch
2 tablespoons tapioca flour
1 teaspoon xanthan gum
1/2 teaspoon baking powder

1/2 teaspoon baking soda
1/2 teaspoon salt
2/3 cup buttermilk or 1 tablespoon lemon juice or reconstituted Ener-G yeast-free/gluten-free vinegar with enough milk (cow, rice, soy, or nut) to equal 2/3 cup
1 teaspoon gluten-free vanilla extract
cooking spray

TOPPING
1/4 cup brown sugar, dried cane juice, or maple or date sugar
1/2 teaspoon cinnamon
1 tablespoon canola, safflower, or other oil
2 tablespoons brown rice flour

Preheat oven to 350 degrees. Coat 11 x 7-inch nonstick pan with cooking spray.

Using an electric mixer and a large mixer bowl, cream together the oil, sugar, and eggs on medium speed until eggs are very fluffy, about 1 minute. Add the grated peel.

In a medium bowl, combine the flours, xanthan gum, baking powder, baking soda, and salt. In another medium bowl, combine the buttermilk and vanilla.

On low speed, beat the dry ingredients into the egg mixture, alternating with the milk mixture, beginning and ending with the dry ingredients. Mix just until combined. Spoon batter into pan and sprinkle topping on top.

Bake 35 minutes or until top is golden brown and cake tester comes out clean.

Preparation = 1 hour. Serves 10.

Coffee Cake Without Fruit — Exchanges

Calories	Fat	% Fat Cal	Protein	Carbohydrate	Cholesterol	Sodium	Fiber	Carbohydrate	Meat	Fat
255	9 g	30 %	3 g	42 g	42 mg	209 mg	1 g	3		2

*Sugar Alternative #1: 3/4 cup fructose powder in place of 3/4 cup granulated sugar
*Sugar Alternative #2: 1/2 cup honey in place of 3/4 cup granulated sugar. Decrease milk to 1/2 cup.
Blueberry-Lemon or Cranberry-Orange Coffeecake: Prepare batter as directed and spread 2/3 of batter in pan, scatter 1 cup chopped blueberries or cranberries on top, and cover with remaining batter. Add topping. Bake as directed. (If using frozen blueberries or cranberries, be sure to drain thoroughly before adding to batter.)

QUICK BREAD

(can be made without wheat, gluten, dairy, or refined sugar - see page 9 about ingredients)

Quick breads are so easy and provide a flavorful addition to breakfast, brunch, or snack time. Use different fruits for variation.

1 cup white or brown rice flour
1/2 cup potato starch
1/2 cup tapioca flour
1 teaspoon xanthan gum
1 teaspoon unflavored gelatin powder
2 1/2 teaspoons baking powder
3/4 teaspoon salt
1/4 teaspoon soy lecithin granules
1/3 cup sugar (cane, unbleached cane, or fructose powder)

1/4 cup canola, safflower, or other oil
2 large eggs, lightly beaten
1 teaspoon gluten-free vanilla extract
3/4 cup milk (cow, rice, soy, or nut)
grated peel from 1 lemon or orange (see below for variations)
fruit (see below)
cooking spray

Preheat oven to 375 degrees. Coat three 5 x 2 1/2-inch nonstick pans with cooking spray. Set aside.

Place dry ingredients in large mixing bowl. Make well in center.

In another bowl, combine oil, eggs, vanilla, milk, and peel. Pour into well of flour mixture. Stir just until ingredients are moistened. Gently stir in fruit (see below). Spoon dough into prepared pans.

Bake for 25-30 minutes (add 5 minutes if using frozen blueberries) or until tops are lightly browned. Remove from oven. Makes 3 small loaves.

Preparation = 40 minutes. Serves 12.

One slice								Exchanges		
Calories	Fat	% Fat Cal	Protein	Carbohydrate	Cholesterol	Sodium	Fiber	Carbohydrate	Meat	Fat
200	6 g	28 %	3 g	35 g	32 mg	229 mg	1 g	2 1/4		1

Blueberry-Lemon Bread: Add lemon peel from 1 lemon and 1 1/4 cups fresh or frozen blueberries.

Cranberry-Orange Bread: Add 1 tablespoon grated orange peel and 1 1/4 cups chopped cranberries.

PANCAKES

(can be made without wheat, gluten, dairy, or refined sugar - see page 9 about ingredients)

These pancakes are light, yet filling. You can freeze the extras.

1 large egg
1/2 cup nonfat plain yogurt*
1/4 cup brown rice flour**
2 tablespoons potato starch
2 tablespoons tapioca flour
1 teaspoon baking powder

1/2 teaspoon baking soda
1 teaspoon sugar or 1/2 teaspoon honey
1/2 teaspoon salt
1 teaspoon gluten-free vanilla extract
1 tablespoon canola, safflower, or other oil
additional oil for frying

Blend egg and yogurt (or milk) in blender or whisk vigorously in bowl. Add remaining ingredients and blend, just until mixed.

Over medium heat, place large, nonstick skillet that has been lightly coated with oil. Pour batter into skillet and cook until tops are bubbly (3-5 minutes). Turn and cook until golden brown (2-3 minutes). Makes about eight 4-inch pancakes. This recipe can be doubled.

Preparation = 15 minutes. Serves 4 (2 per serving).

Per 2 pancakes:

Calories	Fat	% Fat Cal	Protein	Carbohydrate	Cholesterol	Sodium	Fiber	Exchanges Carbohydrate	Meat	Fat
150	5 g	29 %	4 g	23 g	46 mg	417 mg	<1 g	1 1/2		1

*Dairy Alternative: 1/3 cup milk (cow, rice, soy, or nut) in place of 1/2 cup yogurt
**Flour Alternative: 1/4 cup bean flour (from Authentic Foods) in place of 1/4 cup brown rice flour.

PANCAKES WITHOUT EGGS

(can be made without wheat, gluten, dairy, eggs, or refined sugar - see page 9 about ingredients)

Just as good as those without eggs, your egg-sensitive family or friends will appreciate fresh pancakes—hot from the grill.

2/3 cup milk (cow, rice, soy, or nut)
1 teaspoon Ener-G Egg Replacer powder
1/4 cup brown rice flour*
1/4 cup potato starch
1 tablespoon tapioca flour
1 1/4 teaspoons baking powder

3/4 teaspoon baking soda
1 teaspoon sugar or 1/2 teaspoon honey
1/2 teaspoon salt
1 teaspoon gluten-free vanilla extract
1 tablespoon canola, safflower, or other oil
additional oil for frying

Blend milk and Egg Replacer powder in blender until frothy, about 1 minute. Add remaining ingredients and blend, just until mixed.

Over medium heat, place large, nonstick skillet that's been lightly coated with oil. Pour batter into skillet and cook until tops are bubbly (2-3 minutes). Turn and cook until golden brown (1-2 minutes). Makes about eight 4-inch pancakes. Recipe may be doubled.

Preparation = 15 minutes. Serves 4 (2 per serving).

Per 2 pancakes:

| | | | | | | | | Exchanges | | |
Calories	Fat	% Fat Cal	Protein	Carbohydrate	Cholesterol	Sodium	Fiber	Carbohydrate	Meat	Fat
155	5 g	30%	2 g	25 g	6 mg	637 mg	<1 g	1 3/4		1

*Flour Alternative 1/4 cup bean flour (from Authentic Foods) in place of 1/4 cup brown rice flour.

SCONES

(can be made without wheat, gluten, dairy, or refined sugar - see page 9 about ingredients)

Scones resemble large biscuits, usually baked in rounds or wedges. They are extremely versatile. This recipe is so simple and fail-proof. Try it with currants or in a savory fashion with herbs, spices, cheese or meats. (See Variations on next page.)

1/4 cup butter or oleo or canola oil spread (Spectrum™) or canola, safflower, or other oil
2/3 cup yogurt*
1 large egg
2 tablespoons sugar or 1 tablespoon honey
1 1/4 cups brown rice flour
1/2 cup tapioca flour
1 teaspoon xanthan gum

1/4 teaspoon soy lecithin granules
1/2 teaspoon salt
1 1/2 teaspoons cream of tartar
3/4 teaspoon baking soda
1/2 cup currants (optional - avoid if you're sensitive to yeast or mold)
cooking spray

Preheat oven to 425 degrees. Coat nonstick baking sheet with cooking spray. Set aside.

In food processor, blend butter or canola oil spread, yogurt or milk, and egg together until well mixed. Add sugar, flours, xanthan gum, lecithin, salt, cream of tartar, and baking soda. Blend just until mixed. Gently fold in currants. (You may have to transfer mixture to another bowl to successfully blend in currants.) Work quickly so the leavening agent doesn't lose its power. Dough will be soft.

Transfer dough to baking sheet, patting with spatula into 8-inch circle, 3/4-inch thick. Bake for 15-20 minutes or until deeply browned. For crispier, wedge-shaped pieces, cut into 8 wedges and return to oven for final 5 minutes of baking.

Preparation = 25 minutes. Serves 8.

Calories	Fat	% Fat Cal	Protein	Carbohydrate	Cholesterol	Sodium	Fiber	Exchanges Carbohydrate	Meat	Fat
250	7 g	25 %	4 g	44 g	38 mg	334 mg	2 g	3		1 1/2

*Dairy Alternative: 1/2 cup milk (rice, soy or nut) in place of 2/3 cup yogurt

Scones Without Eggs: Omit egg, increase milk to 3/4 cup. If using yogurt, increase to 1 cup. Bake as directed.

FLAVORED SCONES

Ham and Sage Scones: Reduce sugar to 1 tablespoon. After dough is assembled, gently but quickly fold in 1/2 cup finely chopped ham and 1 1/2 teaspoons dried sage. Bake as directed. Serves 8.

| | | | | | | | | Exchanges | | |
Calories	Fat	% Fat Cal	Protein	Carbohydrate	Cholesterol	Sodium	Fiber	Carbohydrate	Meat	Fat
230	7 g	27 %	5 g	38 g	38 mg	334 mg	2 g	2 1/2		1 1/2

Rosemary, Black Olive, & Tomato Scones: Reduce sugar to 1 tablespoon. After dough is assembled, gently but quickly fold in 1 teaspoon crushed dried rosemary leaves, 1/2 cup chopped black olives, and 1/2 cup chopped sun-dried tomatoes. Bake as directed. Serves 8.

| | | | | | | | | Exchanges | | |
Calories	Fat	% Fat Cal	Protein	Carbohydrate	Cholesterol	Sodium	Fiber	Carbohydrate	Meat	Fat
246	8 g	29 %	6 g	38 g	43 mg	449 mg	2 g	2 1/2		1 1/2

Cheese Scones: Reduce sugar to 1 tablespoon. After dough is assembled, gently but quickly fold in 3/4 cup finely shredded Cheddar cheese (cow or soy) and 1/2 teaspoon cayenne pepper. Bake as directed. (Avoid this version if you're sensitive to yeast.) Serves 8.

| | | | | | | | | Exchanges | | |
Calories	Fat	% Fat Cal	Protein	Carbohydrate	Cholesterol	Sodium	Fiber	Carbohydrate	Meat	Fat
272	11 g	34 %	7 g	38 g	49 mg	399 mg	2 g	2 1/2		2 1/4

WAFFLES

(can be made without wheat, gluten, dairy, or refined sugar - see page 9 about ingredients)

Waffles are a special treat for breakfast. Make a whole batch, then freeze any leftovers for another morning. Warm them in the oven (wrapped in foil) or pop them in the toaster.

1 cup brown rice flour*
1/2 cup potato starch
1/4 cup tapioca flour
2 teaspoons baking powder
1 teaspoon salt
1 tablespoon granulated sugar or
   2 teaspoons honey
2 large eggs

2 tablespoons canola, safflower, or other oil
1 1/3 cups buttermilk or 1 tablespoon
   cider vinegar or Ener-G yeast-free/
   gluten-free vinegar (reconstituted) with
   enough milk (cow, rice, soy, or nut) to
   equal 1 1/3 cups
1 teaspoon gluten-free vanilla extract
cooking spray

Heat waffle iron and coat with cooking spray. In a small bowl, sift together flours, baking powder, salt, and sugar. (Add honey, if using, with liquid ingredients.)

Beat eggs well in a large bowl. Add oil, buttermilk, vanilla extract, and the sifted dry ingredients. Beat just until blended.

Pour 1/4 of the batter onto the heated waffle iron. Follow manufacturer's directions. Close and bake until steaming stops, about 4-6 minutes. Repeat with remaining batter. Makes 6 waffles, 6 inches each (depending on size of waffle iron).

Preparation = 30 minutes. Serves 6 (1 waffle per serving).

Per waffle:

| | | | | | | | | Exchanges | | |
Calories	Fat	% Fat Cal	Protein	Carbohydrate	Cholesterol	Sodium	Fiber	Carbohydrate	Meat	Fat
280	8 g	25 %	6 g	48 g	64 mg	523 mg	1 g	3 1/4		1 1/4

*Flour Alternative: 1 cup bean flour (from Authentic Foods) in place of 1 cup brown rice flour.

WAFFLES WITHOUT EGGS

(can be made without wheat, gluten, dairy, eggs, or refined sugar - see page 9 about ingredients)

Even without eggs, these waffles are crisp and delicious. Like their egg-containing counterparts, these waffles freeze well. Re-heat them in the oven (wrapped in foil) or pop them in the toaster.

1 cup brown rice flour*
1/2 cup potato starch
1/4 cup tapioca flour
1 teaspoon baking soda
1 teaspoon salt
1/2 teaspoon xanthan gum
1 tablespoon granulated sugar or
  2 teaspoons honey

2 tablespoons canola, safflower, or other oil
1 1/4 cups buttermilk or 1 tablespoon
  cider vinegar or Ener-G yeast-free/
  gluten-free vinegar (reconstituted)
  with enough milk (cow, rice, soy or
  nut) to equal 1 1/4 cups
1 teaspoon gluten-free vanilla extract
cooking spray

Heat waffle iron and coat with cooking spray. In a small bowl, mix together flours, baking soda, salt, xanthan gum, and sugar. (If using honey, add to liquid ingredients.) Whisk in oil, milk, and vanilla extract just until blended.

Pour 1/4 of the batter onto the heated waffle iron. Follow manufacturer's directions for your particular waffle iron. Close and bake until steaming stops, about 4-6 minutes. Repeat with remaining batter. Makes 6 waffles, 6 inches each.

Preparation = 30 minutes. Serves 6 (1 waffle per serving).

Per waffle:

| | | | | | | | | Exchanges | | |
Calories	Fat	% Fat Cal	Protein	Carbohydrate	Cholesterol	Sodium	Fiber	Carbohydrate	Meat	Fat
260	6 g	22 %	4 g	47 g	4 mg	595 mg	1 g	3		1 1/4

*Flour Alternative: 1 cup bean flour (from Authentic Foods) in place of 1 cup brown rice flour.

COOKING GRAINS

For many of us, hot cereal is an absolute necessity at breakfast—summer, winter, spring, or fall. Just because you don't eat wheat or gluten doesn't mean you can't have cooked cereal. There are many other grains to cook for breakfast besides wheat or oatmeal.

The following table shows you how to cook these alternative grains. I like to stir in a teaspoon of gluten-free vanilla to the cooked cereal—just to boost the flavor. Use salt as you wish. Look on the label for nutrient content.

Grain (1 cup)	Water	Approximate Cooking Time
Amaranth*	2 cups	20-25 minutes
Brown rice	2 1/2 cups	50-55 minutes
Buckwheat*	2 cups	15-20 minutes
Millet*	2 1/2 cups	35-45 minutes
Oats*	2 cups	10-15 minutes
Polenta (Corn) also called Grits	4 cups	10 minutes
Quinoa*	2 cups	15-20 minutes
Wild Rice	4 cups	40 minutes
White Rice	2 cups	20 minutes

Many stores carry quick-cooking versions of some cereals such as buckwheat or rice. Of course, brown rice comes in a 10-minute version, also. Or if you want to "speed up" the cooking process of the larger whole grains (such as brown rice or buckwheat), try whirling them in a blender first. This breaks down the fiber a bit, allowing the grains to cook more quickly.

Favorite toppings for hot cereal include cinnamon, honey, maple syrup, pancake syrup, brown sugar, fresh fruit, fruit-only jam, jelly, or fruit sauces. If you're trying to grow accustomed to the taste and texture of certain cereals (for example, amaranth, quinoa, buckwheat, and millet), combining them with small amounts of cooked brown or white rice may help.

Generally speaking, 1/2 cup of cooked cereal equals one carbohydrate exchange, with these exceptions: Millet = 1/4 cup and Rice = 1/3 cup.

*Amaranth, millet, oats, and quinoa are not recommended for persons with celiac disease. Buckwheat is somewhat controversial, but make sure it is not contaminated with problem grains.

BAGELS

(can be made without wheat, gluten, dairy, or refined sugar - see page 9 about ingredients)

Like all baked goods, these are best eaten on the same day you make them, although they freeze just fine. Warm before eating.

1 cup white rice flour (or bean flour
   from Authentic Foods)
3/4 cup brown rice flour
3/4 cup potato starch
1/2 cup cornstarch
1 tablespoon gluten-free dry yeast
1 tablespoon xanthan gum
1 teaspoon salt
1 cup warm water (105°)
2 tablespoons canola, safflower, or other oil

2 tablespoons honey
1 large egg, lightly beaten
1 teaspoon cider vinegar
cooking spray
cornmeal for baking sheet (optional)
egg white beaten to foam (optional egg wash)

CINNAMON BAGELS
2 teaspoons cinnamon
1/2 cup raisins

Combine flours, cornstarch, yeast, xanthan gum, and salt (and cinnamon, if using) in large mixer bowl. Add water, oil, honey, egg, and vinegar. Beat with electric mixer (using regular beaters) until well blended. Continue mixing on medium for 2 minutes. Mixture will be very thick and stiff. (Add raisins at this point, if using.)

Place dough on flat, floured surface and dust dough with rice flour to make it easier to handle. Divide dough into 8 equal portions. Dust each portion with rice flour, shape each portion into ball, then flatten to 3-inch circle and punch hole in center—continuing to dust with flour, if necessary. Form into bagel shapes (turning rough edges of dough to underside) and place bagels on large baking sheet coated with cooking spray.

Place baking sheet in cold oven, then turn to 325 degrees. Bake for 15 minutes.

Meanwhile, bring 3 inches of water and 1 teaspoon sugar to boil in a deep skillet. Boil bagels on each side for 30 seconds. (Leave oven on.) Using slotted spoon, return bagels to baking sheet that has been coated again with cooking spray (and dusted with the optional cornmeal). Brush with optional egg wash, if desired, to produce a shinier, crispier crust.

Return baking sheet to oven and increase temperature to 400 degrees. Bake bagels for 20-25 minutes, or until nicely browned. Remove bagels and cool on wire rack. Makes 8.

Preparation = 1 1/4 hours. Serves 8.

| | | | | | | | | Exchanges | | |
Calories	Fat	% Fat Cal	Protein	Carbohydrate	Cholesterol	Sodium	Fiber	Carbohydrate	Meat	Fat
270	5 g	16 %	5 g	52 g	23 mg	279 mg	2 g	3 1/2		1

(Raisins add 30 calories and 8 carbohydrate grams to each bagel. If using bean flour, add 3 protein grams.)

RAISIN BREAD

(can be made without wheat, gluten, dairy, or refined sugar - see page 9 about ingredients)

Eat this wonderful breakfast bread plain or with butter, jam or cream cheese. Note different yeast amounts for bread machine versus hand version. Ingredients should be at room temperature.

gluten-free dry yeast (see specific instructions)
1 cup water (see specific instructions)
1 1/3 cups brown rice flour
1/2 cup potato starch
1/4 cup tapioca flour
1 teaspoon xanthan gum
1 teaspoon unflavored gelatin powder
1/3 cup dry milk powder or non-dairy milk powder
1/4 teaspoon soy lecithin granules
1 teaspoon salt

1 teaspoon Ener-G Egg Replacer powder
1/4 cup brown sugar (packed) or dried cane juice or maple sugar
1 teaspoon ground cinnamon
2 large eggs at room temperature
3 tablespoons canola, safflower, or other oil
1 teaspoon cider vinegar or 1/4 teaspoon unbuffered Vitamin C crystals
1/2 cup dark raisins or currants (golden raisins are not recommended)
cooking spray

HAND METHOD: Make sure ingredients are at room temperature for best rising. Combine **1 tablespoon yeast** and 2 teaspoons of the brown sugar in 1 cup warm water (105°). Set aside until foamy, about 5 minutes.

In larger mixer bowl, using regular beaters (not dough hooks), combine flours, xanthan gum, gelatin, dry milk powder, lecithin, salt, Egg Replacer, remaining brown sugar, and cinnamon in large mixer bowl. Add eggs, oil, cider vinegar, and yeast mixture.

Mix ingredients together on low speed until liquid is incorporated, then increase mixer speed to high and beat for 2 minutes. Occasionally, scrape sides of bowl with spatula. Stir in raisins.

For smaller loaves, coat three small pans, 5 x 2 1/2-inches, with cooking spray. Divide dough among pans, smooth tops with spatula, and put in warm place to rise for 35-40 minutes or until doubled in bulk.

For one large loaf, use 9 x 5-inch nonstick pan coated with cooking spray. Place dough in pan, smooth top with spatula, and let dough rise in warm place until double in bulk, 35-40 minutes.

Preheat oven to 350 degrees. Bake the small loaves for about 20-25 minutes; large loaves require about 45 minutes. Cool 5 minutes, then remove from pan. Cool on wire rack.

BREAD MACHINE: Use **1 1/2 teaspoons yeast**. Follow bread machine instructions. I combine dry ingredients and add to bread machine. Combine liquid ingredients (eggs whisked thoroughly; all ingredients at room temperature, including water - 80°). Pour over dry ingredients in bread machine. Set controls and bake. Add raisins following machine instructions. Makes a 1-pound loaf.

Preparation = 3 hours. Serves 10.

Calories	Fat	% Fat Cal	Protein	Carbohydrate	Cholesterol	Sodium	Fiber	Exchanges Carbohydrate	Meat	Fat
215	6 g	24 %	6 g	35 g	37 mg	244 mg	2 g	2 1/4		1 1/4

ENGLISH MUFFINS

(can be made without wheat, gluten, dairy, or refined sugar - see page 9 about ingredients)

English Muffins are surprisingly easy to make. Try them in Eggs Benedict. (See next page.)

2 tablespoons gluten-free dry yeast
2 1/3 cups brown rice flour
2 cups tapioca flour
2/3 cup dry milk powder or non-dairy milk powder
3 teaspoons xanthan gum
1 tablespoon unflavored gelatin powder

1 teaspoon salt
1 tablespoon granulated sugar or honey
1/4 cup canola, safflower, or other oil
4 large egg whites at room temperature
1 1/4 cups warm water (105°)
1 tablespoon yellow cornmeal
cooking spray

Make sure all ingredients are at room temperature.

In large mixer bowl, combine yeast, flours, dry milk powder, xanthan gum, gelatin powder, salt, and sugar (or honey). Blend on low speed, then add oil and egg whites. Mix well. Add warm water and beat on high speed for 3 minutes.

Arrange muffin rings on baking sheet that's been sprayed with cooking spray and dusted with cornmeal. (See page 29 for making your own aluminum foil rings or use 8 ounce pineapple cans with both ends removed.) Spray insides of rings with cooking spray.

Divide dough into 12 equal pieces and press into each ring. Cover and let rise in a warm place for about 50 minutes.

Preheat oven to 350 degrees. Bake the muffins for 15 minutes or until lightly browned. With spatula, turn the muffins (tins and all) over and bake another 10 minutes or until lightly browned. Remove English muffins from baking sheet to cool. When rings are cool enough to handle, remove muffins from rings. Makes 12 English muffins.

Preparation = 1 1/2 hours. Serves 12 (1 muffin each).

Calories	Fat	% Fat Cal	Protein	Carbohydrate	Cholesterol	Sodium	Fiber	Exchanges Carbohydrate	Meat	Fat
270	5 g	17%	5 g	54 g	1 mg	224 mg	1 g	3 1/2		1

*Dairy Alternative: 2/3 cup tapioca flour in place of 2/3 cup dry milk powder

EGGS BENEDICT

(can be made without wheat, gluten, dairy, or refined sugar - see page 9 about ingredients)

Use your own homemade English Muffins in this dish. It features Canadian bacon (lower fat than ham) and a low-fat Hollandaise Sauce.

4 **English Muffins (See page 70)**
8 **pieces thinly-sliced Canadian bacon**
8 **large poached eggs**
1 1/3 **cups Hollandaise Sauce (See page 132)**

1/4 **cup fresh chopped parsley or 2 table-**
   spoons dried parsley
paprika (for garnish)

Make the Hollandaise Sauce. Keep warm in double boiler.

Warm the sliced English Muffins (in microwave or wrapped in foil in a 250-degree oven.)

Meanwhile, warm the Canadian bacon in the microwave to desired serving temperature. Poach eggs.

Arrange two halves of an English Muffin on each of 4 plates. Top each half with a slice of Canadian Bacon, then a poached egg. Top with Hollandaise Sauce, paprika, and parsley.

Preparation = 30 minutes (assumes English Muffins are already made). Serves 4.

Calories	Fat	% Fat Cal	Protein	Carbohydrate	Cholesterol	Sodium	Fiber	Exchanges		
								Carbohydrate	Meat	Fat
620	27 g	39 %	34 g	62 g	569 mg	1533 mg	2 g	4		5

DESSERTS

Life is uncertain. Eat dessert first. — Unknown

Desserts are the "frosting on the cake", the grand finale to a wonderful meal. You'll find a variety of wonderful cakes and cheesecakes, bars, cookies, pies, and fruit desserts in this chapter. None contain wheat or gluten and almost all can be further customized to exclude eggs and dairy products. None use yeast as the leavening agent.

Why are desserts important? If food is a symbol of our relationships, then desserts are the most symbolic of all. For example, we have birthday cakes, the bride and groom cut the wedding cake. We take cakes to new neighbors, grieving families, and potluck dinners.

A word about sugar. We expect desserts to be sweet (that's why we like them!), but not all of us can use refined sugar (especially cane sugar) to achieve that sweetness. So each dish can be made with refined sugar, but all recipes also include instructions for using alternative sweeteners, if you wish. Most of us eat too much sugar. So why not try these dishes using the alternative sweetener options suggested. You might be pleasantly surprised. Plus, see the Appendix for a special section on how to bake with alternative sweeteners.

Cakes & Frostings

See page 9 for information on the special ingredients used in these recipes.

Cookies & Bars

Pies

Fruit Desserts

Cheesecakes

Puddings

Ice Cream

Sauces

BASIC CAKE (WHITE OR YELLOW)

(can be made without wheat, gluten, dairy, or refined sugar - see page 9 about ingredients)

A good yellow cake is an absolute essential for so many recipes. An egg-free version is on the next page. For a white cake, use 3 large egg whites. For a yellow cake, use 2 large eggs.

6 tablespoons butter or oleo or canola oil spread (Spectrum™) or 1/4 cup canola, safflower, or other oil
1 cup granulated sugar*
2 large eggs (or 3 egg whites)
1 tablespoon grated lemon peel
1 cup white or brown rice flour
6 tablespoons potato starch
2 tablespoons tapioca flour
1 teaspoon xanthan gum

1/4 teaspoon baking powder
1/4 teaspoon baking soda
1/3 teaspoon salt
3/4 cup buttermilk or 2 teaspoons lemon juice or reconstituted Ener-G yeast-free/gluten-free vinegar with enough milk (cow, rice, soy, or nut) to equal 3/4 cup
1 teaspoon gluten-free vanilla extract
cooking spray

Preheat oven to 325 degrees. Coat 9 x 5-inch loaf pan or two 5 x 2 1/2-inch pans (or other pans - see below) with cooking spray. (Cake rises better in smaller pans.) Set aside.

Using an electric mixer and a large mixer bowl, cream together the oil, granulated sugar (or fructose), and eggs on medium speed until thoroughly blended. Add grated lemon peel.

In a medium bowl, combine the flours, xanthan gum, baking powder, baking soda, and salt. In another medium bowl, combine the buttermilk (and fruit juice concentrate, if using - see below) and vanilla. On low speed, beat the dry ingredients into the egg mixture, alternating with the buttermilk, beginning and ending with the dry ingredients. Mix just until combined. Spoon batter into pan(s).

Bake the 9 x 5-inch loaf for 50-55 minutes; 35-45 minutes for smaller pans or until top is golden brown and a toothpick inserted into center comes out clean. Cool cake in pan for 5 minutes, then remove from pan and cool on rack. Serves 12.

Preparation = 1 1/4 hours for loaf cake; 35 minutes for cupcake; 50 minutes for layer cake.

| | | | | | | | | Exchanges | | |
Calories	Fat	% Fat Cal	Protein	Carbohydrate	Cholesterol	Sodium	Fiber	Carbohydrate	Meat	Fat
215	8 g	32 %	2 g	35 g	31 mg	118 mg	<1 g	2 1/4		2

*Sugar Alternative #1: 1 cup fructose powder in place of 1 cup granulated sugar
*Sugar Alternative #2: 2/3 cup fruit juice concentrate (thawed but not reconstituted) in place of 1 cup granulated sugar and reduce milk to 1/2 cup. Increase baking soda to 1/2 teaspoon. This version produces a decidedly less sweet cake. Look for *pure* juice concentrate (e.g., white grape, orange, pineapple, or apple).

Cupcakes: Bake 12 cupcakes for 20- 25 minutes or until firm.
Layer Cake: Bake in a 9-inch round nonstick pan for 35-40 minutes or two 8-inch round nonstick pans for 30 minutes. Be sure to line pans with waxed paper or parchment paper and spray with cooking spray for easy cake removal. Cool on wire rack.

BASIC CAKE WITHOUT EGGS

(can be made without wheat, gluten, dairy, eggs, or refined sugar - see page 9 about ingredients)

This cake was designed for people who can't eat eggs. It can be baked as a loaf cake, cupcakes, layer cake, or used for Pineapple Upside-Down Cake or any dessert requiring a basic cake.

1 cup white or brown rice flour
1/2 cup potato starch
1/4 cup tapioca flour
1/2 teaspoon xanthan gum
2 1/4 teaspoons baking powder
1/4 teaspoon salt
3/4 cup granulated sugar*

1/2 cup butter or oleo or canola oil
    spread (Spectrum™) or 1/3 cup
    canola, safflower, or other oil
2 teaspoons gluten-free vanilla extract
1/2 cup soft silken tofu by Mori-Nu®
    grated lemon peel of 1 lemon
1/2 cup boiling water
    cooking spray

Preheat oven to 350 degrees and lightly coat a 9 x 5-inch nonstick loaf pan (or two 5 x 2 1/2-inch pans - or other pan sizes, see below) with cooking spray. (Cake rises better in smaller pans.) Sift together the flours, xanthan gum, baking powder, and salt. Set aside.

In a food processor, cream together the sugar, butter at room temperature (or canola oil spread or oil), vanilla, tofu, and lemon peel. Process on high until completely smooth and glossy. Add boiling water and process on high until completely mixed. Add flour mixture and process until smooth. Scrape down sides of bowl with spatula, if necessary.

Spoon batter into prepared pan(s) and bake 9 x 5-inch pan for 1 hour; small pans for 30-40 minutes or until tops are firm. Cake will not brown. Remove from oven and cool for 10 minutes before removing from pan(s). Cool completely before cutting.

Preparation = 1 hour, 10 minutes for 9 x 5-inch loaf; 40-50 minutes for 5 x 2 1/2-inch loaves. Serves 12.

Calories	Fat	% Fat Cal	Protein	Carbohydrate	Cholesterol	Sodium	Fiber	Exchanges Carbohydrate	Meat	Fat
215	8 g	34 %	2 g	35 g	20 mg	191 mg	<1 g	2 1/2		1 1/4

(Using Spectrum™ subtracts 20 cholesterol grams.)

*Sugar Alternative: 2/3 cup honey or pure maple syrup in place of 3/4 cup granulated sugar. Reduce boiling water to 1/3 cup. Add 1/4 teaspoon baking soda. Reduce oven to 325 degrees.

Cupcakes: Bake 12 standard-size cupcakes for 20-25 minutes or until tops are firm.
Layer Cake: Line an 8 or 9-inch round nonstick pan with waxed paper and spray with cooking spray. Spread batter in pan and bake at 350 degrees for 35-40 minutes or until top is firm. Or, bake in two 8-inch round nonstick pans for 20 minutes or until tops are firm. Cool cake for 10 minutes before removing from pan. Cool on wire rack.

BASIC CAKE MIX

(can be made without wheat, gluten, dairy, or refined sugar - see page 9 about ingredients)

This mix will come in handy if you make the Basic Cake often. Store in an airtight container in a dry, dark place for up to 3 months. This mix will make 4 recipes.

4 cups granulated sugar or fructose powder	4 teaspoons xanthan gum
4 cups white or brown rice flour	1 teaspoon baking powder
1 1/2 cups potato starch	1 teaspoon baking soda
1/2 cup tapioca flour	1 1/4 teaspoons salt

Combine ingredients in airtight container and store in dark, dry place.

To make one Basic Cake recipe:

Preheat oven to 325 degrees. Coat 9 x 5-inch or two 5 x 2 1/2-inch nonstick pans with cooking spray. Set aside.

With electric mixer, cream together the following in a large mixing bowl on medium speed until thoroughly blended:

6 tablespoons butter at room temperature or Spectrum™ canola oil spread or 1/4 cup canola, safflower, or other oil

2 large eggs (or 3 large egg whites)

1 tablespoon grated lemon peel

In another medium bowl, combine 3/4 cup buttermilk (see page 75 for buttermilk substitute) and 1 teaspoon gluten-free vanilla extract. Add 2 1/2 cups plus 2 tablespoons Basic Cake mix to egg mixture alternately with milk, beginning and ending with dry ingredients. Mix until well combined. Spoon batter into pan(s).

Bake large loaf for 50-55 minutes, small pans for 35-40 minutes or until tops are golden brown and a cake tester comes out clean. Cool cake in pan for 5 minutes, then remove from pan and cool on rack. Serves 12.

Lemon Poppy Seed Cake: Increase lemon peel to 2 tablespoons and add 2 tablespoons poppy seed. Bake as directed.

See page 75 for nutrient content and exchanges.

CARROT CAKE

(can be made without wheat, gluten, dairy, or refined sugar - see page 9 about ingredients)

This version of the popular carrot cake derives extra flavor and texture from pineapple, coconut, and nuts. Top it with the conventional cream cheese frosting or simply dust with powdered sugar if you want it to be dairy-free.

1 1/2 cups brown rice flour
1/2 cup potato starch
1/2 cup soy or bean flour
1 teaspoon xanthan gum
2 teaspoons baking soda
2 teaspoons cinnamon
1 teaspoon salt
1/2 teaspoon ground ginger
4 large eggs
1 cup brown sugar, packed*
1 cup granulated sugar*
1/3 cup canola, safflower, or other oil
1 cup low-fat plain yogurt**

1 teaspoon gluten-free vanilla extract
3 cups shredded carrots
1 1/2 cups crushed pineapple, drained
1 cup shredded coconut
1 cup walnuts, chopped
cooking spray

FROSTING (optional)
3 ounces cream cheese (1/3 cup), softened
2 cups powdered sugar
2 tablespoons milk (cow, rice, soy, or nut)
1 teaspoon gluten-free vanilla extract

Preheat oven to 350 degrees. Spray 10-cup Bundt pan with cooking spray. Combine flours, xanthan gum, baking soda, cinnamon, salt, and ginger together in a bowl. Set aside.

In large mixer bowl, beat together the eggs, sugars, oil, yogurt, and vanilla. Add flour mixture slowly until just blended. With a large spatula, stir in carrots, pineapple, coconut, and nuts. Pour batter into prepared pan.

Bake 45-50 minutes or until toothpick inserted in center of cake comes out clean. Cool on wire rack. Remove cake from pan. Frost with Cream Cheese Frosting.

CREAM CHEESE FROSTING: Combine softened cream cheese, powdered sugar, milk, and vanilla. Beat until smooth.

Preparation = 1 1/4 hours. Serves 12.

One slice without frosting: Exchanges

Calories	Fat	% Fat Cal	Protein	Carbohydrate	Cholesterol	Sodium	Fiber	Carbohydrate	Meat	Fat
330	6 g	16 %	7 g	64 g	61 mg	452 mg	3 g	4 1/4		1 1/4

One slice with frosting: Exchanges

Calories	Fat	% Fat Cal	Protein	Carbohydrate	Cholesterol	Sodium	Fiber	Carbohydrate	Meat	Fat
415	6 g	13 %	7 g	85 g	61 mg	459 mg	3 g	5 3/4		1 1/4

*Sugar Alternative #1: 1 cup dried cane juice or maple sugar instead of 1 cup brown sugar
*Sugar Alternative #2: 1 cup fructose powder in place of 1 cup granulated sugar
**Dairy Alternative: 3/4 cup non-dairy milk (rice, soy, or nut) in place of yogurt

CHOCOLATE CAKE

(can be made without wheat, gluten, dairy, or refined sugar - see page 9 about ingredients)

This is a very versatile dessert. Serve it plain, with a dusting of powdered sugar, or your favorite frosting. Save the leftovers and crumble them into crusts for pies or cheesecakes.

1/2 cup brown rice flour
1/2 cup potato starch
1/4 cup tapioca flour
1/2 cup unsweetened cocoa (not Dutch)
1 teaspoon xanthan gum
1 1/4 teaspoons baking soda
3/4 teaspoon salt
1 cup brown sugar*

2 teaspoons gluten-free vanilla extract
1/2 cup milk (cow, rice, soy, or nut)
1/2 cup butter or canola oil spread
   (Spectrum™) or 1/3 cup canola,
   safflower, or other oil
1 large egg
3/4 cup hot brewed coffee or hot water
cooking spray

Preheat oven to 350 degrees. Coat 9 x 9-inch round or square or 11 x 7-inch nonstick pan with cooking spray. Set aside.

Place all ingredients, except hot water or coffee, in large bowl and blend with electric mixer. Add hot water or coffee and mix until thoroughly blended. Pour into prepared pan and bake for 30-35 minutes or until toothpick placed in center of cake comes out clean.

Cupcakes: Bake 12 cupcakes for 20-25 minutes or until toothpick comes out clean.

Layer Cake: Bake in a 9-inch round nonstick pan for 30-35 minutes or two 8-inch round nonstick pan for 25-30 minutes or until toothpick inserted in center comes out clean. Be sure to line pan(s) with waxed paper or parchment paper and spray with cooking spray for easier cake removal.

Preparation = 45 minutes. Serves 12. (Can double recipe in 13 x 9-inch pan.)

Calories	Fat	% Fat Cal	Protein	Carbohydrate	Cholesterol	Sodium	Fiber	Exchanges Carbohydrate	Meat	Fat
200	9 g	38 %	2 g	30 g	37 mg	355 mg	2 g	2		2 1/2

*Sugar Alternative #1: 1 cup dried cane juice or maple sugar in place of brown sugar. Add 1/4 teaspoon baking soda.

*Sugar Alternative #2: 2/3 cup maple syrup in place of 1 cup brown sugar. Add 1/4 teaspoon baking soda. Decrease coffee or water to 1/2 cup.

CHOCOLATE CAKE WITHOUT EGGS

(can be made without wheat, gluten, dairy, eggs, or refined sugar - see page 9 about ingredients)

This can be used just like the Chocolate Cake on the previous page. The great news is that it doesn't contain eggs, yet has a texture so fabulous that you'd never guess the eggs are missing. Using fruit puree helps reduce the fat content, but if you'd rather not use pureed fruit just increase the oil to 1/2 cup.

1/2 cup brown rice flour
1/2 cup potato starch
1/4 cup tapioca flour
1/2 cup cocoa powder (not Dutch)
1/2 teaspoon xanthan gum
2 1/4 teaspoons baking powder
1/2 teaspoon salt
3/4 cup brown sugar*

1/4 cup butter or oleo or canola oil
   spread (Spectrum™) or canola,
   safflower, or other oil
1/4 cup prune puree or applesauce
   or 1 jar of baby food prunes or
   applesauce (2.5 ounces)
1/4 cup soft silken tofu
2 teaspoons gluten-free vanilla
2/3 cup boiling hot coffee or water
cooking spray

Preheat oven to 350 degrees. Lightly coat a 9-inch round or square nonstick pan (may use 8-inch springform pan) with cooking spray. Combine the flours, cocoa, xanthan gum, baking powder, and salt. Set aside.

In a food processor, cream together the sugar, oil (or butter or oleo, which should be at room temperature), and prunes (or applesauce) until smooth. Add tofu and vanilla. Process on high until completely smooth. Add boiling coffee (or water) and process on high until completely mixed. Add flour mixture and process until smooth.

Spoon batter into prepared pan and bake for 25-30 minutes or until top is firm and toothpick inserted in center comes out clean. Remove from oven and cool for 5 minutes before removing from pan (if using springform pan).

Preparation = 45 minutes. Serves 12.

								Exchanges		
Calories	Fat	% Fat Cal	Protein	Carbohydrate	Cholesterol	Sodium	Fiber	Carbohydrate	Meat	Fat
150	5 g	25 %	2 g	28 g	10 mg	190 mg	2 g	2		1

(Using Spectrum™ reduces cholesterol by 10 grams.)

Sugar Alternative #1: 3/4 cup dried cane juice or maple sugar instead of 3/4 cup brown sugar. Add 1/4 teaspoon baking soda.

Sugar Alternative #2: 2/3 cup honey or pure maple syrup in place of brown sugar. Reduce hot coffee or water to 1/3 cup. Add 1/4 teaspoon baking soda. Reduce oven to 325 degrees.

CHOCOLATE FUDGE TORTE WITHOUT EGGS

(can be made without wheat, gluten, dairy, eggs, or refined sugar - see page 9 about ingredients)

This cake is adapted from the winning recipe in a recent contest. This version captures all the delicious decadence of the original—without the offending ingredients!

CAKE

1/2 cup brown rice or bean flour (from Authentic Foods)
1/4 cup potato starch
1/4 cup tapioca flour
1/2 cup unsweetened cocoa (not Dutch)
1/2 teaspoon xanthan gum
3/4 teaspoon baking soda
1/2 teaspoon baking powder
3/4 teaspoon salt
2 teaspoons ground cinnamon

1 cup brown sugar*
1 teaspoon Egg Replacer (by Ener-G)
1/3 cup cooking oil
2 teaspoons gluten-free vanilla
16 ounces canned pears, drained
1/3 cup hot strongly brewed coffee
1/2 cup chopped nuts (macadamia or pecan) — optional
2 teaspoons water

FILLING
1/4 cup milk (cow, rice, soy, or nut)
1/2 cup dairy-free chocolate chips
cooking spray

CHOCOLATE FUDGE SAUCE or CHOCOLATE FROSTING
(See Index)

FILLING: In small saucepan, combine milk and chocolate over low heat and stir until smooth. (Or melt in microwave, stirring until smooth.) Set aside.

CAKE: Preheat oven to 325 degrees. Spray 8-inch nonstick springform pan with cooking spray. Set aside. In large bowl, mix flours, cocoa, xanthan gum, baking soda, baking powder, salt, cinnamon, brown sugar, and Egg Replacer together with oil and vanilla until thoroughly mixed. Mixture will be dry and crumbly. Set aside 1/2 cup of the mixture. In blender or food processor, puree drained pears. (Use juice for another purpose.)

In large bowl, thoroughly mix dry cake mixture, pureed pears, and hot coffee with electric mixer. Spread batter in prepared pan. Spoon filling onto top of batter. Stir nuts and 2 teaspoons water into remaining 1/2 cup dry cake mixture and sprinkle over filling.

Bake for 50 minutes or until top of cake center springs back when touched lightly. Cool in pan on wire rack for 10 minutes. Remove from pan. Let cool completely.
Preparation = 1 1/4 hours. Serves 12.

| | | | | | | | | Exchanges | | |
Calories	Fat	% Fat Cal	Protein	Carbohydrate	Cholesterol	Sodium	Fiber	Carbohydrate	Meat	Fat
295	13 g	37 %	4 g	47 g	1 mg	244 mg	4 g	3		2 3/4

*Sugar Alternative: 1 cup dried cane juice or maple sugar in place of brown sugar. Increase baking soda by 1/4 teaspoon.

Chocolate Fudge Torte With Eggs: Use 2 large eggs in place of 1/3 cup hot coffee. Bake as directed.

FLOURLESS CHOCOLATE TORTE

(can be made without wheat, gluten, dairy, or refined sugar - see page 9 about ingredients)

This torte avoids flour altogether and is moderately decadent! If only all restaurants had at least one dessert like this for their wheat-sensitive customers!

2/3 cup brown sugar, packed*	4 egg whites at room temperature
3 ounces dairy-free chocolate	1/4 teaspoon cream of tartar
1/2 cup unsweetened Dutch cocoa	1 teaspoon gluten-free vanilla extract
1/3 cup boiling water	1/2 teaspoon gluten-free almond extract
2 egg yolks at room temperature	1 teaspoon honey
3/4 cup almonds or pecans, finely ground	cooking spray
1 teaspoon xanthan gum	

Preheat oven to 375 degrees. Line bottom of 8-inch nonstick springform pan with waxed paper or parchment paper. Spray parchment paper and sides of pan with cooking spray.

Combine brown sugar (reserve 1 tablespoon), chocolate, cocoa, and boiling water in small bowl. Stir until chocolate is melted. Whisk in egg yolks.

Finely grind almonds or pecans in food processor. Add xanthan gum.

Using electric mixer, beat egg whites and cream of tartar until soft peaks form. Add reserved tablespoon of brown sugar and beat until stiff, but not dry. Carefully whisk nut mixture into chocolate mixture, adding vanilla and almond extract. Fold in egg whites in two additions.

Transfer batter to prepared pan. Place pan in larger pan of boiling water so that water comes up one inch on outer sides of springform pan.

Bake for 35 minutes or until toothpick inserted into center comes out clean. Cool torte in pan on rack. Cut around edge of torte to loosen from pan edges. Release pan sides. Slice into 10 pieces.

Preparation = 45 minutes. Serves 10.

								Exchanges		
Calories	Fat	% Fat Cal	Protein	Carbohydrate	Cholesterol	Sodium	Fiber	Carbohydrate	Meat	Fat
170	8 g	37 %	5 g	25 g	53 mg	38 mg	3 g	1 3/4		1 3/4

Sugar Alternative: 2/3 cup dried cane juice or maple sugar in place of 2/3 cup brown sugar. Dissolve dried cane juice or maple sugar in the recipe's 1/3 cup boiling water before adding to recipe.

GINGERBREAD

(can be made without wheat, gluten, dairy, or refined sugar - see page 9 about ingredients)

Dense, moist, and flavorful, this gingerbread is further enhanced by a tangy Lemon Sauce.

1/4 cup canola, safflower, or other oil
1/2 cup brown sugar, packed*
1 large egg
1/2 cup molasses
1 teaspoon gluten-free vanilla extract
3/4 cup brown rice flour
1/2 cup potato starch
1/4 cup tapioca flour
1 teaspoon baking soda
1 1/2 teaspoons ground ginger
3/4 teaspoon cinnamon
1/2 teaspoon cloves
1/2 teaspoon salt
1/2 cup buttermilk or 1 teaspoon
   cider vinegar or Ener-G yeast-free/
   gluten-free vinegar (reconstituted)
   plus enough milk (cow, rice, soy,
   or nut) to make 1/2 cup

LEMON SAUCE
1/4 cup granulated sugar or 3 tablespoons honey
1 tablespoon cornstarch or arrowroot
1/8 teaspoon salt
1/2 cup water
2 teaspoons grated lemon peel
1 tablespoon fresh lemon juice
1 teaspoon canola, safflower, or other oil
cooking spray

Preheat oven to 350 degrees. In large bowl, cream oil and brown sugar with electric mixer. Add egg, molasses, and vanilla and beat well. Mix flours with baking soda, ginger, cinnamon, cloves, and salt. Add flour mixture alternately with buttermilk to creamed mixture. Pour into 8 or 9-inch round or square nonstick pan that has been coated with cooking spray.

Bake for 30 minutes or until a toothpick inserted into center comes out clean. Cool pan on wire rack.

Preparation = 45 minutes. Serves 12.

One slice without Lemon Sauce:

Calories	Fat	% Fat Cal	Protein	Carbohydrate	Cholesterol	Sodium	Fiber	Exchanges Carbohydrate	Meat	Fat
150	5 g	29 %	2 g	25 g	15 mg	215 mg	<1 g	1 1/2		1

Lemon Sauce: In small saucepan, combine sugar, cornstarch, and salt until blended. Gradually stir in 1/2 cup water. Cook and stir over medium heat until mixture boils and thickens. Stir in lemon peel, lemon juice, and oil. Serve warm over Gingerbread. (If using honey, dissolve cornstarch in 2 tablespoons of the water first, then add honey and salt. Proceed with directions.) (Adds 50 calories and 10 carbohydrate grams per serving.)

*Sugar Alternative: 1/3 cup pure maple syrup or honey in place of 1/2 cup brown sugar. Reduce buttermilk to 1/3 cup. Increase baking soda to 1 1/4 teaspoons.

GINGERBREAD WITHOUT EGGS

(can be made without wheat, gluten, dairy, eggs, or refined sugar - see page 9 about ingredients)

Very flavorful, this gingerbread is ideal for persons who can't eat eggs.

1 cup brown rice flour
2/3 cup potato starch
2 tablespoons tapioca flour
1 teaspoon xanthan gum
1 teaspoon baking powder
3/4 teaspoon baking soda
1 tablespoon ground ginger
1 teaspoon cinnamon
1/2 teaspoon ground cloves
1/4 teaspoon ground nutmeg
3/4 teaspoon salt
1/2 cup brown sugar (packed) or dried cane
    juice—or 1/3 cup honey or pure maple syrup
1 cup boiling water

1/2 cup soft silken tofu by Mori-Nu®
1 teaspoon gluten-free vanilla extract
1/3 cup molasses
1/4 cup canola, safflower, or other oil
cooking spray

LEMON SAUCE:
3 tablespoons honey
1/2 cup water
1/8 teaspoon salt
1 tablespoon cornstarch or arrowroot
2 teaspoons grated lemon peel
1/2 teaspoon gluten-free vanilla extract

Preheat oven to 325 degrees. Spray 9-inch round nonstick pan with cooking spray. Measure flours, xanthan gum, baking powder, baking soda, ginger, cinnamon, cloves, nutmeg, and salt into small bowl. Set aside.

In a food processor, puree the sugar (or dried cane juice, honey or maple syrup), boiling water (reduce to 2/3 cup if using honey or maple syrup), tofu, vanilla, and molasses until very, very smooth. Add oil and blend thoroughly. Add flours and process until just blended. Batter will be somewhat thick. Pour batter into prepared pan.

Bake 30-35 minutes or until toothpick inserted in center comes out clean. Remove from oven. Cool thoroughly before slicing. Serve with Lemon Sauce.

Preparation = 45 minutes. Serves 12.

One slice without Lemon Sauce:

| | | | | | | | | Exchanges | | |
Calories	Fat	% Fat Cal	Protein	Carbohydrate	Cholesterol	Sodium	Fiber	Carbohydrate	Meat	Fat
200	5 g	24 %	2 g	37 g	0 mg	250 mg	1 g	2 1/2		1 1/2

Lemon Sauce: Whisk together the honey, all but 2 tablespoons of the water, and salt in small, heavy saucepan over low-medium heat. In separate small bowl, whisk cornstarch (or arrowroot) with remaining 2 tablespoons water to form smooth paste. Stir paste into honey mixture, whisking constantly until mixture comes to gentle boil. Remove from heat and stir in lemon rind and vanilla. Serve warm over Gingerbread. (Adds 50 calories and 10 carbohydrate grams per serving.)

NOTE: If using honey or maple syrup in Gingerbread, increase baking soda to 1 teaspoon.

PINEAPPLE UPSIDE-DOWN CAKE

(can be made without wheat, gluten, dairy, eggs, or refined sugar depending on the Basic Cake recipe used - see page 9 about ingredients)

This family favorite is so easy when you use either of the Basic Cake recipes in this chapter.

1 recipe Basic Cake or Basic Cake Without Eggs (page 75-76)
1/2 cup brown sugar, packed*
16 ounces pineapple rings in juice, drained

7 maraschino cherries (optional—or use raspberries or sliced strawberries)
cooking spray

Preheat oven to 350 degrees.

In a 10-inch pie plate or skillet (or special pan designed for upside-down cake), spray with cooking spray. Evenly sprinkle brown sugar (or dried cane juice) over bottom of pan. Arrange pineapple slices with maraschino cherry (or raspberries or strawberries) in center of each circle. Pour cake batter evenly on top.

Bake 40-45 minutes or until top springs back when touched. Cool 5 minutes, then invert onto serving plate.

Preparation = 45 minutes. Serves 12.

Nutritional Data Based on Basic Cake recipe (with eggs):

Calories	Fat	% Fat Cal	Protein	Carbohydrate	Cholesterol	Sodium	Fiber	Carbohydrate	Meat	Fat
410	8 g	17 %	3 g	85 g	30 mg	180 mg	2 g	5 3/4		2

Exchanges

*Sugar Alternative: 1/2 cup dried cane juice or maple sugar in place of 1/2 cup brown sugar

SPICE CAKE

(can be made without wheat, gluten, dairy, or refined sugar - see page 9 about ingredients)

The spicy flavors of this delicious cake combine very well with the Coffee 7-Minute Frosting (page 89.) This cake is a real winner among students in my cooking classes!

1 cup brown rice flour*
2/3 cup potato starch
1/3 cup tapioca flour
1 teaspoon xanthan gum
1 3/4 teaspoons baking soda
3/4 teaspoon salt
1 tablespoon ground ginger
2 teaspoons ground cinnamon
1/2 teaspoon ground nutmeg

1/4 teaspoon ground cloves
1 1/2 cups milk (cow, rice, soy, or nut)
1 1/2 cups brown sugar**
1/2 cup canola, safflower, or other oil
1/3 cup molasses
1 teaspoon gluten-free vanilla extract
2 large eggs, beaten
cooking spray
Coffee 7-Minute Frosting (See page 89)

Preheat oven to 325 degrees. Coat a 9-inch round nonstick cake pan or two 8-inch round cake pans with cooking spray. Line bottom with waxed paper or parchment paper, then spray again. Set aside.

Sift together the flours, xanthan gum, baking soda, salt, ginger, cinnamon, nutmeg, and cloves in a large mixing bowl. Set aside.

Combine milk and sugar in heavy saucepan and bring just to a boil over medium heat. Remove from heat and add oil, molasses, and vanilla extract. Cool slightly.

Add cooled mixture to flour mixture in mixing bowl and mix with electric mixer until thoroughly blended. Add eggs and mix well. Pour batter into prepared pan(s).

Bake 9-inch pan for 50-55 minutes or 8-inch pans for 35-40 minutes or until toothpick inserted in center of cake comes out clean. Cool cake in pan for 5 minutes. Invert the cake(s) onto a wire rack or plate to finish cooling and remove waxed paper.

Preparation = 1 1/4 hours. Serves 12.

One slice without frosting:

Calories	Fat	% Fat Cal	Protein	Carbohydrate	Cholesterol	Sodium	Fiber	Carbohydrate	Meat	Fat
265	8 g	25 %	2 g	50 g	4 mg	344 mg	1 g	3 1/4		1 1/2

Exchanges (above right of table)

*Flour Alternative: 1 cup bean flour (from Authentic Foods) in place of 1 cup brown rice flour

**Sugar Alternative: 1 1/2 cups dried cane juice or maple sugar in place of 1 1/2 cups brown sugar. Dissolve dried cane juice or maple sugar in the recipe's 1 1/2 cups hot milk before adding to cake. Add 1/4 teaspoon baking soda.

SPICE CAKE WITHOUT EGGS

(can be made without wheat, gluten, dairy, eggs, or refined sugar - see page 9 about ingredients)

The soft silken tofu replaces eggs and yields a moist, fragrant layer cake that fills your kitchen with an intoxicating aroma. Top the cake with your favorite frosting. For an interesting taste, try using brewed coffee as the liquid for the frosting.

1 cup brown rice flour
2/3 cup potato starch
2 tablespoons tapioca flour
1 teaspoon xanthan gum
1 teaspoon baking powder
3/4 teaspoon baking soda
3/4 teaspoon salt
2 teaspoons ground ginger
2 teaspoons ground cinnamon

1/4 teaspoon ground nutmeg
1/4 teaspoon ground cloves
1 cup boiling water
3/4 cup brown sugar, packed*
1/2 cup soft silken tofu by Mori-Nu®
1/2 cup molasses
1 teaspoon gluten-free vanilla extract
1/4 cup canola, safflower, or other oil
cooking spray

Preheat oven to 325 degrees. Spray 9-inch round nonstick pan or two 8-inch round nonstick pans with cooking spray. Line with waxed paper and spray again. Set aside.

In a large mixing bowl, sift together dry ingredients. Set aside.

Dissolve brown sugar (or dried cane juice or maple sugar) in 2/3 cup boiling water (reserving remaining 1/3 cup of water). Set aside.

In a food processor, puree the tofu, dissolved sugar/water mixture, molasses, and vanilla. (If using honey or maple syrup, add now.) Puree until very, very smooth.

Add flour mixture and process just until mixed. Add remaining 1/3 cup boiling water and oil. Blend until mixed. You may have to scrape sides of food processor bowl with spatula. Batter will be somewhat thick. Pour batter into prepared pan(s).

Bake 9-inch pan for 40-45 minutes or 8-inch pans for 30-35 minutes or until toothpick inserted into center comes out clean. Remove from oven. Cool in pan for 10 minutes, then carefully remove and cool cake(s) on wire rack. Cool completely before frosting or cutting. Frost with preferred frosting or top with your favorite sauce.

Preparation = 50-60 minutes. Serves 12.

| One slice without frosting | | | | | | | | Exchanges | | |
Calories	Fat	% Fat Cal	Protein	Carbohydrate	Cholesterol	Sodium	Fiber	Carbohydrate	Meat	Fat
215	5 g	22 %	2 g	40 g	0 mg	250 mg	1 g	2 1/2		1

*Sugar Alternative #1: 3/4 cup dried cane juice or maple sugar in place of the 3/4 cup brown sugar. Increase baking soda to 1 teaspoon.

*Sugar Alternative #2: 1/2 cup honey or maple syrup in place of the 3/4 cup brown sugar. Reduce boiling water to 3/4 cup. Increase baking soda to 1 teaspoon.

CHOCOLATE FROSTING

(can be made without wheat, gluten, dairy, eggs, or refined sugar - see page 9 about ingredients)

Chocoholics—indulge yourself with this decadent-tasting frosting, knowing that it contains no refined sugar or eggs. It is soft, but "sets up" with a lovely, glossy sheen.

3 ounces (1/3 cup) extra-firm silken tofu
   by Mori-Nu®
1 cup pure maple syrup

1 tablespoon vanilla
1 cup unsweetened cocoa (not Dutch)
1/8 teaspoon salt

   In food processor, blend tofu, maple syrup, and vanilla extract until very, very smooth. Add cocoa and salt and process until smooth. Mixture will be very soft, but firms up after refrigerating. Refrigerate for 15 minutes before using.

Preparation = 25 minutes (includes chilling time). Frosts cake for 12.

| | | | | | | | | Exchanges | | |
Calories	Fat	% Fat Cal	Protein	Carbohydrate	Cholesterol	Sodium	Fiber	Carbohydrate	Meat	Fat
175	2 g	10 %	3 g	45 g	0 mg	13 mg	5 g	3		1/2

COFFEE 7-MINUTE FROSTING

(can be made without wheat or gluten - see page 10. This recipe contains eggs.)

If you've ever wondered why some frostings look so beautifully shiny with elegant dips and swirls, chances are they were 7-Minute Frostings made with eggs and sugar. Using substitutions for the eggs and granulated sugar (or fructose powder) is not successful, so if you cannot eat these two ingredients you might try your favorite frosting recipe, instead.

1 teaspoon gluten-free instant coffee powder	1/4 teaspoon cream of tartar
1 teaspoon very hot water or brewed coffee	3 tablespoons cold water
3 large egg whites	1 teaspoon gluten-free vanilla extract
1 1/4 cups granulated sugar or fructose powder	

Dissolve instant coffee crystals in very hot water or hot brewed coffee. Set aside.

In double boiler over simmering water, combine egg whites, granulated sugar, cream of tartar, and cold water. (Bottom of double boiler should not touch water.) Beat with portable electric mixer for 7 minutes. Remove from heat and stir in vanilla extract and coffee liquid, and beat with a spatula until glossy and desired spreading consistency is reached. Use immediately.

To frost a layer cake, spread about 3/4 cup of the frosting on the bottom half of cake. Place top half of cake on bottom half and frost sides and top. Top with optional garnishes of your choice including shaved chocolate, Dutch cocoa powder, or chopped nuts.

Preparation = 10 minutes. Frosts a cake for 12.

								Exchanges		
Calories	Fat	% Fat Cal	Protein	Carbohydrate	Cholesterol	Sodium	Fiber	Carbohydrate	Meat	Fat
85 g	<1 g	<1 %	<1 g	20 g	0 mg	17 mg	0 g	1 1/4		

FLUFFY FROSTING

(can be made without wheat, gluten, dairy, or refined sugar - see page 9 about ingredients)

Fluffy and irresistible, this frosting is so elegant it can be used on the most special occasions. This recipe requires a candy thermometer, so be sure you have one. Also, you need to work quickly once the frosting is ready, so have the cake completely assembled before starting the frosting. For safety sake, use only fresh eggs and refrigerate the frosted cake.

1 cup pure maple syrup	1 teaspoon gluten-free vanilla extract
2 large egg whites (room temperature)	1/8 teaspoon salt

Place maple syrup in heavy, narrow saucepan and attach a candy thermometer to edge of saucepan. (Be sure to follow manufacturer's directions for your candy thermometer.) Cook syrup over low-medium heat until it registers 239 degrees, stirring occasionally.

Meanwhile (while syrup boils), in a large mixing bowl of an electric stand mixer, beat egg whites and salt until peaks form. As soon as the syrup reaches 239 degrees, begin to drip it very slowly into the egg whites, continuing to beat with the mixer until icing begins to thicken. It is ready when it falls off a spatula in a thin, threadlike fashion. Stir in vanilla.

With a spatula, ice the cake immediately with wide, sweeping movements around the sides and top.

Preparation = 30 minutes. Frosts cake for 12.

								Exchanges		
Calories	Fat	% Fat Cal	Protein	Carbohydrate	Cholesterol	Sodium	Fiber	Carbohydrate	Meat	Fat
90	0 g	0 %	1 g	22 g	0 mg	23 mg	0 g	1 1/4		

BASIC COOKIE

(can be made without wheat, gluten, dairy, eggs, or refined sugar - see page 9 about ingredients)

These little cookies taste great and they're indispensable—they travel well, they make great crumb crusts for pies, and they can be crumbled over puddings and fruit desserts. If you want a very crisp cookie, then omit the egg white. The optional grated lemon peel adds a delightful taste.

1/4 cup butter or canola oil spread
  (Spectrum™) or oleo
2 tablespoons honey
1/2 cup granulated sugar*
1 1/2 teaspoons gluten-free vanilla extract
3/4 cup brown rice flour
1/2 cup white rice flour
3 tablespoons potato starch
2 tablespoons tapioca flour

1/2 teaspoon xanthan gum
1/2 teaspoon salt
1 1/2 teaspoons baking powder
1 large egg white
2 teaspoons grated lemon peel (optional)
2 tablespoons water or more (if not using
  food processor to mix dough or if omitting
  egg)
cooking spray

In food processor, combine the butter (room temperature, but not melted), honey, sugar, and vanilla. Add the flours, xanthan gum, salt, baking powder, and egg white, blending until mixture forms large clumps. (If using electric mixer, blend butter, honey, sugar, vanilla, and egg white until fluffy. Add dry ingredients and blend thoroughly. Add water if needed, 1 tablespoon at a time.) Shape into ball, cover and refrigerate for 1 hour.

Preheat oven to 325 degrees.

Using one-half of dough at a time, roll to 1/4-inch thickness between sheets of waxed paper or plastic wrap which are sprinkled with rice flour. Keep remaining dough chilled until ready to use. Spray baking sheet with cooking spray. Cut into desired shapes and transfer to baking sheet, placing 1 inch apart.

Bake at 325 degrees for 10-12 minutes or until edges are set. Switch position of pan(s) half-way through baking for even heat distribution.

Remove from oven and cool two minutes before transferring to rack to cool. Decorate with favorite icing** after cookies are cooled. Makes 16.

Preparation = 30 minutes (excludes chilling time). Serves 16.

Per Cookie: Exchanges

Calories	Fat	% Fat Cal	Protein	Carbohydrate	Cholesterol	Sodium	Fiber	Carbohydrate	Meat	Fat
122	4 g	28 %	1 g	22 g	0 mg	105 mg	<1 g	1 1/2		3/4

*Sugar Alternative: 1/2 cup fructose powder in place of 1/2 cup sugar

** Be sure to read labels of purchased frostings or mixes. Many contain wheat or gluten.

See next page for variations and special tips on making cut-out cookies.

BASIC COOKIE VARIATIONS

These variations may be used with the Basic Cookie recipe on the previous page or the Vanilla Wafer recipe on page 98.

ANISE-PINE NUT COOKIES: Add 1 teaspoon gluten-free anise flavoring and 1/2 cup toasted finely chopped pine nuts. Bake as directed. (Nuts add 17 calories, 2 fat grams, and 2 protein grams per serving.)

SPICE COOKIES: Add 1/4 teaspoon freshly ground nutmeg, 1/2 teaspoon ground cinnamon, and 1/8 teaspoon ground cloves. Bake as directed.

PECAN COOKIES: Add 1/2 cup finely chopped pecans, 1 teaspoon each gluten-free pecan extract and butter extract (optional), and 1/8 teaspoon baking soda. Bake as directed. (Nuts add 15 calories, 2 fat grams, and 2 protein grams per serving.)

LEMON POPPYSEED COOKIES: Add 2 tablespoons poppy seeds and 2 tablespoons grated lemon peel. Bake as directed.

TIPS FOR SUCCESSFUL "CUT-OUT" COOKIES

1. To avoid sticking, use non-stick baking liners or parchment paper.

2. Insulated baking sheets assure even baking and won't buckle.

3. Metal cookie cutters work better than plastic cookie cutters.

4. If the chilled dough is too stiff to roll, leave dough at room temperature for 15-20 minutes. Then knead dough with hands so your body warmth makes dough more pliable. If dough is too soft after rolling, chill or freeze rolled dough until firm—then cut into desired shapes. For best results, do not roll dough thinner than 1/4 inch.

5. If you're having trouble transferring the cookies to the baking sheet, try rolling the dough onto parchment paper or nonstick liners, cut desired shapes, remove scraps of dough (leaving cut-out cookies on paper) and transfer paper or liner (cookies and all) to baking sheet.

CHOCOLATE WAFERS

(can be made without wheat, gluten, dairy, eggs, or refined sugar - see page 9 about ingredients)

Use these cookies just as you would use the purchased kind—either as a treat in themselves, or crush them into Crumb Crusts (page 100) for pies and cheesecakes. I keep a batch in the freezer, then make them into crumbs with my food processor. For a crisper cookie—much like the chocolate wafers we buy to make crumb crusts—omit the egg.

1/4 cup butter or canola oil spread (Spectrum™) or oleo
2 tablespoons honey
1/2 cup brown sugar, firmly packed*
1 large egg
1 1/2 teaspoons gluten-free vanilla extract
1 cup brown rice flour
3 tablespoons potato starch

2 tablespoons tapioca flour
1/4 cup unsweetened cocoa (not Dutch)
1/2 teaspoon xanthan gum
1/2 teaspoon salt
1 1/2 teaspoons baking powder
cooking spray
additional water, if needed

Preheat oven to 350 degrees.

If using egg: In a large mixing bowl, beat together the butter, honey, sugar, egg, and vanilla. Set aside.

In another bowl, combine the flours, cocoa, xanthan gum, salt, and baking powder. Stir this mixture into the creamed mixture. Cover and refrigerate for 1 hour.

If omitting egg: Blend all ingredients together in food processor. Add additional water, if necessary, 1 tablespoon at a time. Shape the batter into a soft ball. Cover and refrigerate for 1 hour.

Dust hands with cocoa powder (or cooking spray) and shape dough into 1-inch balls. Place on cookie sheet that has been coated with cooking spray. Flatten slightly with bottom of glass dipped into cocoa powder or sprayed with cooking spray.

Bake for about 30 minutes or until cookies appear dry on top. Makes about 24 cookies.

Preparation = 45 minutes. Serves 24.

Per Cookie:

								Exchanges		
Calories	Fat	% Fat Cal	Protein	Carbohydrate	Cholesterol	Sodium	Fiber	Carbohydrate	Meat	Fat
75	3 g	32 %	1 g	12 g	8 mg	71 mg	<1 g	3/4		1/2

*Sugar Alternative: 1/2 cup dried cane juice or maple sugar in place of 1/2 cup brown sugar

CHOCOLATE CHIP COOKIES

(can be made without wheat, gluten, dairy, or refined sugar - see page 9 about ingredients)

Everybody's favorite. Now you can enjoy these treats along with everyone else. For chocolate chip bars, bake the dough in an 8 x 8-inchsquare pan for 25-30 minutes or until golden brown.

3/4 cup brown rice flour
1/2 cup tapioca flour
1/4 cup potato starch
1/2 teaspoon baking soda
1 teaspoon xanthan gum
1/4 teaspoon salt
1/4 cup butter, canola oil spread
    (Spectrum™), or oleo

3/4 cup brown sugar, packed*
5 tablespoons granulated sugar**
2 teaspoons gluten-free vanilla extract
1 extra large egg
1 cup dairy-free chocolate chips
1/4 cup chopped walnuts (optional)
cooking spray

Preheat oven to 350 degrees. Mix together flours, baking soda, xanthan gum, and salt. Set aside. Coat a 13 x 9-inch baking sheet with cooking spray. Set aside.

In large mixer of bowl, beat butter (or canola oil spread or oleo at room temperature) with brown sugar, granulated sugar, vanilla extract, and egg, scraping sides of bowl frequently. Beat in flour mixture on low speed, mixing thoroughly. Stir in chocolate chips (and nuts, if using). Drop by tablespoonfuls on baking sheet. (If you are using canola oil spread, the cookies won't spread as they bake. You must press them down to a thickness of 1/2-inch with your palm or the bottom of a drinking glass. Use your fingers to shape the cookie to a perfect circle.)

Bake on center rack of oven for 10-12 minutes or until lightly browned. Cool for 2-3 minutes before removing from cookie sheet. Makes 24 cookies.

Preparation = 25 minutes. Serves 24.

Per Cookie:

								Exchanges		
Calories	Fat	% Fat Cal	Protein	Carbohydrate	Cholesterol	Sodium	Fiber	Carbohydrate	Meat	Fat
120	5 g	34 %	1 g	20 g	8 mg	76 mg	<1 g	1 1/4		1

*Sugar Alternative #1: 3/4 cup dried cane juice in place of brown sugar. Add 1/4 teaspoon baking soda.

**Sugar Alternative #2: 5 tablespoons fructose powder in place of granulated sugar

CHOCOLATE BROWNIES

(can be made without wheat, gluten, dairy, or refined sugar - see page 9 about ingredients)

Serve these scrumptious brownies plain or with a dusting of powdered sugar. Or, for a really decadent brownie, top with your favorite frosting.

1/2 cup brown rice flour or bean flour (from Authentic Foods)
1/4 cup potato starch
1/4 cup tapioca flour
1/2 cup unsweetened cocoa (not Dutch)
1/2 teaspoon baking powder
1/2 teaspoon salt
1/4 teaspoon xanthan gum
1 teaspoon gluten-free instant coffee powder (optional)

1/4 cup butter or oleo or canola oil spread (Spectrum™) or canola, safflower, or other oil
1/2 cup brown sugar*
1/2 cup granulated sugar*
1 large egg
2 teaspoons gluten-free vanilla
1/4 cup hot water or brewed coffee
1/2 cup chopped walnuts (optional)
cooking spray

Preheat oven to 350 degrees. Spray 8-inch square nonstick pan with cooking spray. Set aside.

Stir together the flours, cocoa, baking powder, salt, xanthan gum, instant coffee (if using), and Egg Replacer. Set aside.

In large mixing bowl, beat the butter (or oil), sugars, egg, and vanilla with electric mixer on medium speed until well combined. With mixer on low speed, add dry ingredients and hot water or coffee. Mix until just blended. Mixture will be somewhat thick. Stir in nuts, if using. Spread batter in prepared pan.

Bake for 20 minutes. Cool brownies before cutting.

Preparation = 30 minutes. Serves 12.

Per Brownie:

| | | | | | | | | Exchanges | | |
Calories	Fat	% Fat Cal	Protein	Carbohydrate	Cholesterol	Sodium	Fiber	Carbohydrate	Meat	Fat
180	6 g	28 %	2 g	33 g	0 mg	109 mg	1.5 g	2		1 1/4

*Sugar Alternative: 1 cup dried cane juice or maple sugar in place of the 1/2 cup brown and 1/2 cup granulated sugar. Add 1/4 teaspoon baking soda.

Chocolate Brownies Without Eggs: Omit egg and add 1 teaspoon Ener-G Egg Replacer powder. Increase hot water or coffee to 1/2 cup. Bake as directed.

"GRAHAM" CRACKERS

(can be made without wheat, gluten, dairy, eggs, or refined sugar - see page 9 about ingredients)

These easy treats are especially nice for children, but adults will find them delicious as well. Crush them for crumb pie crusts.

1/2 cup brown rice flour
1/2 cup soy flour
1/4 cup tapioca flour
1/4 cup potato starch
1/2 teaspoon xanthan gum
1/2 teaspoon salt
1 teaspoon baking powder
3/4 teaspoon cinnamon
1/8 teaspoon mace (optional)

1/8 teaspoon ginger (optional)
1/3 cup brown sugar (packed) or maple sugar or dried cane juice
2 tablespoons honey or molasses
1 teaspoon gluten-free vanilla extract
1/3 cup soft butter or oleo or canola oil spread (Spectrum™)
2 tablespoons water (if needed)
additional water (if not using food processor)
cooking spray

Place all ingredients in a food processor and blend until mixture forms ball. (Or mix ingredients with electric mixer, adding a tablespoon of water at a time until mixture can be shaped into soft ball.) Refrigerate for 1 hour.

Preheat oven to 325 degrees. Coat nonstick baking sheet with cooking spray. Place dough on baking sheet and top with waxed paper or plastic wrap. Pat with your hands or roll to 1/8-inch thickness with a rolling pin or tall glass. Remove paper and cut dough into 3-inch squares using a sharp knife. Prick each square several times with a fork. (Or, roll dough onto parchment paper or nonstick liners, cut squares, and transfer parchment paper or liner—with crackers on them—to baking sheet.)

Bake for 15-20 minutes or until brown, but watch carefully as they burn easily. Remove from oven when browned and run knife along cut lines again. Cool on pan for 2 minutes, then cool on wire rack. Crackers will become crisp as they cool. Makes 24.

Preparation = 1 hour (excludes chilling time). Serves 24.

Per 3-inch square:

Calories	Fat	% Fat Cal	Protein	Carbohydrate	Cholesterol	Sodium	Fiber	Exchanges Carbohydrate	Meat	Fat
70	3 g	35%	1 g	11 g	7 mg	87 mg	<1 g	3/4		1/2

GINGERSNAPS

(can be made without wheat, gluten, dairy, eggs, or refined sugar - see page 9 about ingredients)

These cookies are great for snacking at home, but they also travel very well. Keep some in your freezer to make crumb crusts for pies.

1/4 cup butter or oleo or canola oil spread (Spectrum™)
3 tablespoons molasses
1/2 cup brown sugar, packed*
1 teaspoon gluten-free vanilla extract
3/4 cup brown rice flour
1/2 cup tapioca flour
1/4 cup soy flour
1 teaspoon xanthan gum
1/2 teaspoon salt
1 teaspoon baking powder
1 1/2 teaspoons ground ginger
1 1/2 teaspoons ground cinnamon
1/4 teaspoon ground nutmeg
1/4 teaspoon ground cloves
2 tablespoons water (if needed)
cooking spray

In a food processor, combine butter (room temperature), molasses, sugar, and vanilla. Add dry ingredients and blend until thoroughly mixed together and dough forms a ball. (Add water, 1 tablespoon at a time, only if mixture fails to form a large ball—or if using electric mixer instead of food processor.) Refrigerate for one hour.

Preheat oven to 325 degrees. Spray baking sheet with cooking spray. Set aside. Dust hands with rice flour and shape into 1-inch balls. Place on baking sheet. Flatten slightly with bottom of drinking glass.

Bake for 20-25 minutes, or until cookies start to brown on the bottom. Cool cookies on the cookie sheet for about 5 minutes, then transfer to wire rack to cool. Store in airtight containers. Makes 16 cookies.

Preparation = 45 minutes. Serves 16.

Per cookie:

								Exchanges		
Calories	Fat	% Fat Cal	Protein	Carbohydrate	Cholesterol	Sodium	Fiber	Carbohydrate	Meat	Fat
110	3 g	26 %	1 g	20 g	0 mg	115 mg	<1 g	1 1/4		1/2

(Using Spectrum™ subtracts 8 cholesterol grams.)

***Sugar Alternative:** 1/2 cup dried cane juice or maple sugar in place of 1/2 cup brown sugar

VANILLA WAFERS

(can be made without wheat, gluten, dairy, eggs, or refined sugar - see page 9 about ingredients)

Use these cookies as you would use the commercial variety. They make excellent crusts for cheesecakes or toppings for fruit desserts.

1/4 cup butter or oleo or canola oil spread (Spectrum™)
1/3 cup honey
2 teaspoons gluten-free vanilla extract
1 1/4 cups brown rice flour
1/2 teaspoon salt
1/2 teaspoon xanthan gum
1 1/2 teaspoons baking powder
3 tablespoons potato starch
2 tablespoons tapioca flour
2 tablespoons water (if mixing without food processor)
cooking spray

Preheat oven to 325 degrees.

Blend ingredients in food processor until mixture forms ball. Add water only if necessary (or if mixing by hand). Refrigerate for 1 hour.

With rice floured hands, shape dough into 1-inch balls. Place on cookie sheet that has been sprayed with cooking spray. Flatten to 1/4-inch with bottom of drinking glass.

Bake for about 20-25 minutes, or until cookies are lightly browned. Remove from cookie sheet and cool. Store in airtight container. If cookies harden, place apple slice in container or gently warm in microwave oven. Makes 16.

Preparation = 45 minutes (excludes chilling time). Serves 16.

Per cookie: Exchanges

Calories	Fat	% Fat Cal	Protein	Carbohydrate	Cholesterol	Sodium	Fiber	Carbohydrate	Meat	Fat
100	3 g	27 %	1 g	18 g	8 mg	123 mg	<1 g	2		1/2

NOTE: For a softer cookie, add an egg yolk

PIE CRUST

(can be made without wheat, gluten, dairy, eggs, or refined sugar - see page 9 about ingredients)

You can enjoy pie—even on a special diet. Smaller pie crusts work better with this dough, so an 8-inch pie plate is recommended. If you prefer 9 or 10-inch double-crust pies, just double the recipe. The version using canola oil spread and soft silken tofu is easiest to handle.

1/2 cup brown rice flour
1/2 cup tapioca flour
1/2 teaspoon baking powder
1/2 teaspoon xanthan gum
1/2 teaspoon unflavored gelatin powder
1/4 teaspoon salt

1/4 cup canola oil spread (Spectrum™) or vegetable shortening or oleo
1/4 cup Yogurt Cheese* (See page 142)
2 tablespoons milk (cow, rice, soy, or nut)
1 teaspoon granulated sugar (optional for sprinkling top of crust)

Place all ingredients in food processor and process until mixture forms ball on one side of bowl. (If it does not form ball, it is too dry. Add water, 1 teaspoon at a time, until mixture forms ball.) Remove from food processor and cover. Chill until dough is firm enough to handle easily, about 1 hour.

Roll half of the dough between two rice-floured pieces of waxed paper or plastic wrap. To place in 8-inch pie plate, remove one piece of paper and invert carefully onto plate trying to center dough over plate. (It is difficult to "move" dough so centering the first time is important.) Remove remaining waxed paper and press into place, making sure that dough edges cover rim of pie plate. If dough is difficult to handle, press entire bottom crust in place with your fingers. Fill pie crust with filling of choice.

Roll remaining half of dough between floured sheets of waxed paper. Invert onto filled pie crust, trying to "center" crust as much as possible. Push and pinch the dough (rather than roll or fold) to form ridge around rim of pie plate. Decoratively shape rim. Brush top crust with milk. (Or combine 1 egg white and 1 tablespoon water and brush top with egg mixture.) Sprinkle with granulated sugar, if desired.

Bake as directed—usually 30-40 minutes in 400 degree oven for fruit pies. Don't overbake (especially with the tofu version, since it doesn't brown).

For a baked crust (to fill later, e.g., puddings), bake in preheated 400 degree oven for 25 minutes or until crust is lightly browned.

Preparation = 30 minutes (excluding chilling time). Serves 6.

Made with Yogurt Cheese: Exchanges

Calories	Fat	% Fat Cal	Protein	Carbohydrate	Cholesterol	Sodium	Fiber	Carbohydrate	Meat	Fat
185	8 g	37 %	2 g	29 g	1 mg	188 mg	<1 g	2		1 1/2

(Using tofu subtracts 54 calories, 7 fat grams and 52 sodium mg.)

*Dairy Alternative: 1/4 cup soft silken tofu by Mori-Nu® in place of the 1/4 cup Yogurt Cheese. However, crust will not brown as deeply. Or use 1/2 cup canola oil spread or vegetable shortening and omit the Yogurt Cheese (or tofu).

CRUMB CRUST FOR PIES

(can be made without wheat, gluten, dairy, eggs, or refined sugar - see page 9 about ingredients)

Save a few of the Vanilla Wafers (page 98), Chocolate Wafer Cookies (page 93), or "Graham" Crackers (page 96) to crush for this pie crust. It is great for cheesecakes and no-bake pie fillings such as puddings and custards.

1 cup crushed cookie crumbs (Vanilla Wafer, Chocolate Wafers, or "Graham" Crackers (pages 98, 93, or 96)
2 tablespoons canola, safflower, or other oil

1/4 cup finely chopped nuts (if you prefer to avoid nuts, use 1 1/4 cups cookie crumbs)
1 tablespoon brown sugar*

Combine all ingredients and press into 9-inch microwave-safe pie plate. Cook 2-3 minutes on high until firm. Fill crust with no-bake filling of your choice.
Preparation = 10 minutes. Serves 6.

With nuts:

| | | | | | | | | Exchanges | | |
Calories	Fat	% Fat Cal	Protein	Carbohydrate	Cholesterol	Sodium	Fiber	Carbohydrate	Meat	Fat
200	10 g	46 %	1 g	27 g	11 mg	185 mg	<1 g	1 3/4		2

(Omitting nuts subtracts 15 calories and 2 fat grams.)

*Sugar Alternative: 1 tablespoon honey in place 2 tablespoons brown sugar

CLAFOUTI

(can be made without wheat, gluten, dairy, or refined sugar - see page 9 about ingredients)

This is one of the easiest dishes to make and I've served it for dessert—or for breakfast. A variety of different fruits will work, but stone fruits (peaches or apricots) seem to work best. This dessert is especially good for people who must watch their sugar intake, but you can make it as sweet as your taste buds desire.

3 tablespoons brown rice flour
1 tablespoon potato starch
1/2 teaspoon salt
2 large eggs
1/3 cup milk (cow, rice, soy, or nut)
2 tablespoons honey or pure maple syrup

1 teaspoon gluten-free vanilla extract
1/2 teaspoon grated lemon peel
2 tablespoons canola, safflower, or other oil
3 cups peaches, cut in 1-inch pieces
2 tablespoons powdered sugar (optional)
cooking spray

Preheat oven to 375 degrees.

Combine the flours, salt, eggs, milk, honey, vanilla, and lemon peel in a blender and whirl for one minute on high speed. (An immersion or hand-held blender works well here, but you may also use a wire whisk.) Batter will resemble pancake batter.

Spray one 9-inch, oven proof skillet or pan or 2 small, oven-proof skillets or pans with cooking spray. Pour in 1/4 of the batter, spreading it over the bottom of the pan. Place skillet(s) in oven. Cook until the batter resembles a cooked pancake, about 5-7 minutes.

Remove from heat. Put the fruit on top of the cooked batter. Top with remaining batter.

Bake small skillets for 20-25 minutes; large skillet for 35-40 minutes, or until top is puffy and golden brown. Remove from oven and dust with powdered sugar, if desired. Serve immediately.

Preparation = 45 minutes. Serves 4.

Calories	Fat	% Fat Cal	Protein	Carbohydrate	Cholesterol	Sodium	Fiber	Exchanges Carbohydrate	Meat	Fat
200	10 g	44 %	5 g	24 g	94 mg	307 mg	2 g	1 1/2		2

FRUIT COBBLER

(can be made without wheat, gluten, dairy, or refined sugar - see page 9 about ingredients)

Fresh fruit cobblers are such a treat, nestled under a rich, biscuit blanket. Many fruits will work, but remember that the more tart the fruit, the more sweetener you'll need. Blackberries make the most flavorful version (a personal favorite at our house).

FRUIT FILLING
4 cups blackberries, blueberries, or fruit of
    choice (washed and cut in small pieces)
1/2 cup granulated sugar*
1 tablespoon quick-cooking tapioca
1 teaspoon grated lemon peel
1 tablespoon fresh lemon juice
1 teaspoon gluten-free vanilla extract
cooking spray

COBBLER TOPPING
1/2 cup brown rice flour
1/4 cup potato starch
1/4 cup tapioca flour
1/4 teaspoon xanthan gum
1 teaspoon grated lemon peel
1/2 teaspoon baking soda
1/2 teaspoon baking powder
1/4 teaspoon salt
1/2 cup plain yogurt or 1/4 cup milk (cow,
    rice, soy, or nut)
2 tablespoons lemon juice
2 tablespoons canola, safflower, or other oil
1 teaspoon gluten-free vanilla
1 large egg
1 tablespoon honey or liquid FruitSource®

FRUIT FILLING: Preheat oven to 400 degrees. Spray 8 x 8-inch pan with cooking spray. Combine fruit filling ingredients in prepared pan and set aside.

TOPPING: In large bowl, combine flours, xanthan gum, peel, baking soda, baking powder, and salt. In another bowl, whisk together yogurt (or milk), lemon juice, oil, vanilla, egg, and honey. Add to dry ingredients, stirring just until moistened. Drop by tablespoonfuls onto fruit.

Bake for 20-25 minutes or filling is bubbly and crust is golden. Serve warm.

Preparation = 45 minutes. Serves 6.

Calories	Fat	% Fat Cal	Protein	Carbohydrate	Cholesterol	Sodium	Fiber	Exchanges Carbohydrate	Meat	Fat
290	6 g	18 %	4 g	60 g	30 mg	249 mg	5 g	4		1 1/4

(Omitting egg subtracts 1 protein gram and 30 cholesterol grams.)

*Sugar Alternative: 1/4 cup honey or liquid FruitSource® in place of 1/2 cup granulated sugar

Fruit Cobbler Without Eggs: In cobbler topping, omit egg and use 1/3 cup milk instead of 1/4 cup milk. (If using yogurt, use 2/3 cup instead of 1/2 cup.) Bake as directed.

FRUIT TART

(can be made without wheat, gluten, dairy, eggs, or refined sugar - see page 9 about ingredients)

This dessert looks so spectacular, yet is so simple to make. Plus, it can be made with far fewer calories than a traditional tart and only uses natural sweeteners (if you use preserves that are sweetened with fruit juices only).

1 recipe Pie Crust (See page 99)   **3/4 cup peach fruit-only preserves**
7 canned peach halves, well-drained

Preheat oven to 375 degrees. Press pie crust into 8-inch tart pan (similar to a springform pan with a removable rim). A regular pie pan will work if you don't have a tart pan, but the edges will be more slanted rather than straight up and down. Bake crust for 10 minutes.

Remove from oven. Place peach halves (cut side down) on crust. Top with 3/4 cup melted fruit preserves and brush tops of fruit and pie crust edges with melted preserves. Bake at 375 degrees for 25-30 minutes or until crust is nicely browned. Cool to room temperature before cutting.

Preparation = 45 minutes. Serves 6.

Using Pie Crust made with tofu:

Calories	Fat	% Fat Cal	Protein	Carbohydrate	Cholesterol	Sodium	Fiber	Exchanges Carbohydrate	Meat	Fat
180	<1 g	2 %	2 g	47 g	0 mg	38 mg	4 g	3		

CHEESECAKE (NEW YORK)

(can be made without wheat, gluten, or refined sugar - see page 9 about ingredients)

This tastes just like the authentic New York cheesecake. For variation, top with fresh fruit such as strawberries or blueberries—or add additional lemon or orange peel for a bolder citrus flavor. For a dairy-free cheesecake, see next page.

1 cup Vanilla Wafers (See page 98) or other gluten-free cookies
1 cup low-fat, dry curd cottage cheese
3 large eggs
2 8-ounce packages of low-fat cream cheese, softened
1 teaspoon grated lemon peel

2 tablespoons fresh lemon juice
1 tablespoon tapioca flour
1 cup granulated sugar*
1 1/2 teaspoons gluten-free vanilla extract
1/4 teaspoon salt
cooking spray

CRUST: Spray bottom and sides of 8-inch springform pan with cooking spray. Press crushed Vanilla Wafers (or other gluten-free cookies) onto bottom of pan and slightly up the sides. Chill while preparing filling.

FILLING: Preheat oven to 300 degrees. In food processor, puree cottage cheese and eggs for 3 minutes until cottage cheese is silky smooth. Add remaining ingredients and puree until very smooth. Slowly pour into chilled crust.

Bake for 1 hour or until cheesecake is set. Let cool in pan on wire rack. Cover and chill up to 8 hours or overnight. Remove sides of pan and transfer cheesecake to serving plate. (Garnish with fresh strawberries or raspberries, if desired.)

Preparation = 1 1/4 hours. Serves 12.

Calories	Fat	% Fat Cal	Protein	Carbohydrate	Cholesterol	Sodium	Fiber	Exchanges Carbohydrate	Meat	Fat
255	10 g	35%	8 g	30 g	70 mg	340 mg	<1 g	2		2 1/2

*Sugar Alternative #1: 2/3 cup honey in place of 1 cup granulated sugar. Omit lemon juice.

*Sugar Alternative #2: 1 cup fructose powder in place of 1 cup granulated sugar

CHEESECAKE (NEW YORK) WITHOUT EGGS

(can be made without wheat, gluten, dairy, eggs, or refined sugar - see page 9 about ingredients)

This cheesecake is very easy to assemble—all ingredients are combined in a food processor. Then, simply pour into the crust and chill. It produces a chiffon-like cheesecake, although using real sour cream and Yogurt Cheese (in place of the alternatives) produces a creamier texture. Look for casein-free versions of sour cream alternative and cream cheese alternative.

1 cup crushed Vanilla Wafers (See page 98) or other gluten-free cookies
1 tablespoon honey
2 packets (4 teaspoons) unflavored gelatin powder
1 cup evaporated skim milk (or rice, soy, or nut milk)

3/4 cup granulated sugar*
1 tablespoon gluten-free vanilla extract
2 cups sour cream alternative or cream cheese alternative**
1 cup Yogurt Cheese** (See page 142)
grated lemon peel from 1 lemon
cooking spray

CRUST: In food processor, process the cookies until they are fine crumbs. Add honey and process again. Remove crumbs and press onto bottom and up the sides of 8-inch springform pan which has been coated with cooking spray. Bake at 350 for 10-15 minutes. Set aside.

FILLING: In small saucepan, sprinkle gelatin over milk and allow to soften for one minute. Heat gently over low heat until gelatin is dissolved, about 3 minutes.

In the food processor, process the sugar (or fructose or honey), vanilla, sour cream, and yogurt cheese (or tofu) until very smooth. Add lemon peel and gelatin mixture and pulse until well mixed. Pour into the prepared crust and chill in refrigerator for 3 hours.

To serve, unmold by running knife around edge of pan. Slice with a warm knife. (Garnish with fresh strawberries, raspberries, or lemon slices and sprigs of mint.) Or drizzle Blueberry Sauce (See page 113) over top.

Preparation = 3 1/2 hours (includes 3 hour chilling time). Serves 12.

Calories	Fat	% Fat Cal	Protein	Carbohydrate	Cholesterol	Sodium	Fiber	Exchanges Carbohydrate	Meat	Fat
183	5 g	25 %	5 g	30 g	15 mg	144 mg	<1 g	2		1

*Sugar Alternative #1: 3/4 cup fructose powder in place of 3/4 cup granulated sugar
*Sugar Alternative #2: 1/2 cup honey in place of 3/4 cup granulated sugar. Reduce milk to 3/4 cup.
**Dairy Alternative: 2 cups soft silken tofu by Mori-Nu® in place of sour cream or cream cheese alternative. Use 1 cup soft silken tofu by Mori-Nu® in place of 1 cup Yogurt Cheese.

CHOCOLATE CHEESECAKE

(can be made without wheat, gluten, or refined sugar - see page 9 about ingredients)

One of my tasters called this dessert "rich and yummy" even though it uses low-fat cream cheese and low-fat cottage cheese. Be sure to keep a few Chocolate Wafers (See page 93) on hand for the crust. This dessert is so quick and easy to make in your food processor.

1/4 cup crushed Chocolate Wafers (See page 93)	1 teaspoon gluten-free vanilla extract
16 ounces no-fat cream cheese	1/4 teaspoon salt
1 cup cottage cheese (1% fat)	1 large egg
1 cup brown sugar, packed*	2 tablespoons dairy-free chocolate chips
1/3 cup unsweetened cocoa (not Dutch)	(optional)
1/2 cup tapioca flour	cooking spray
1/4 cup milk (cow, rice, soy, or nut)	

Preheat oven to 300 degrees.

Sprinkle chocolate wafer crumbs in bottom of 8-inch springform pan that has been coated with cooking spray. Set aside.

In food processor, cream together the cream cheese and cottage cheese until very, very smooth. Add brown sugar, cocoa powder, flour, milk, vanilla extract, and salt. Process until smooth. Add egg and blend just until blended. Stir in chocolate chips, if using. Slowly pour mixture over crumbs in pan.

Bake for 1 hour, or until cheesecake is set. Let cool in pan on wire rack. Cover and chill for at least 8 hours or overnight. Remove sides of pan and transfer cake to a serving plate. (Garnish with fresh fruit, if desired.) Makes 10 servings.

Preparation = 1 1/4 hours. Serves 12.

Calories	Fat	% Fat Cal	Protein	Carbohydrate	Cholesterol	Sodium	Fiber	Exchanges Carbohydrate	Meat	Fat
220	10 g	35 %	8 g	30 g	40 mg	265 mg	1 g	2		2

*Sugar Alternative: 1 cup dried cane juice or maple sugar in place of 1 cup brown sugar

CHOCOLATE CHEESECAKE WITHOUT EGGS

(can be made without wheat, gluten, dairy, eggs, or refined sugar - see page 9 about ingredients)

It's hard to believe that cheesecake doesn't have to contain cream cheese or eggs, but this version omits both—if you use the tofu. And, it doesn't require baking. Look for casein-free versions of sour cream alternative or cream cheese alternative.

1 cup crushed Chocolate Wafers (See page 93)
1 tablespoon honey
2 packets (4 teaspoons) unflavored gelatin powder
1 cup evaporated skim milk (or rice, soy, or nut milk)
1/2 cup unsweetened cocoa (not Dutch)
3/4 cup brown sugar*

2 teaspoons gluten-free vanilla extract
1 teaspoon gluten-free instant coffee powder (optional)
2 cups sour cream or cream cheese alternative or 2 cups soft silken tofu by Mori-Nu®
1 cup Yogurt Cheese (See page 142) or soft silken tofu by Mori-Nu®
1 tablespoon grated orange peel (optional)
cooking spray

CRUST: In food processor, process the cookies until they are fine crumbs. Add honey and process again. Remove crumbs and press onto bottom and up the sides of 8-inch springform pan which has been sprayed with cooking spray. Bake at 350 for 10-15 minutes. Set aside.

FILLING: In small saucepan, sprinkle gelatin over milk and allow to soften for one minute. Heat gently over low heat until gelatin is dissolved, about 3 minutes. (If using maple or date sugar, dissolve in warmed milk after the gelatin dissolves.)

In a food processor, combine the cocoa powder, sugar, vanilla, coffee powder (if using), sour cream or cream cheese, and Yogurt Cheese (or tofu) and process until very, very smooth. Add gelatin mixture (and orange peel, if using) and process for 3 minutes or until thoroughly mixed. Scrape sides of bowl down periodically. Pour into the prepared crust and chill for 3 hours.

To serve, unmold and slice with a warm knife. (Garnish with fresh strawberries or raspberries, sprigs of mint, or chocolate shavings, if desired.)

Preparation = 3 1/2 hours (includes chilling time). Serves 12.

Calories	Fat	% Fat Cal	Protein	Carbohydrate	Cholesterol	Sodium	Fiber	Exchanges Carbohydrate	Meat	Fat
190	6 g	25 %	6 g	30 g	15 mg	145 mg	2 g	2		1 1/4

*Sugar Alternative: 3/4 cup dried cane juice, maple sugar or date sugar in place of 3/4 cup brown sugar. For best results, dissolve sugar in warmed milk before adding to recipe.

BUTTERSCOTCH PUDDING

(can be made without wheat, gluten, dairy, eggs, or refined sugar - see page 9 about ingredients)

Extremely rich and satisfying. This is a great dessert because you can make it ahead of time and there's no last minute preparation.

1/2 cup dark brown sugar, packed*	1 large egg yolk (optional)
2 tablespoons cornstarch or sweet rice flour	1 tablespoon butter (optional)
1/4 teaspoon salt	1 teaspoon vanilla
1 1/2 cups evaporated skim milk or 1 1/3 cups milk (cow, rice, soy, or nut)	1/2 teaspoon gluten-free butter-extract (optional)

In a large, heavy saucepan over medium heat, whisk together the sugar, cornstarch or arrowroot, and salt. Add the milk gradually, whisking constantly. Whisk in egg yolk (if using) and bring the mixture to a boil, whisking constantly. Immediately reduce heat to low and continue to boil for another full minute. (This boiling time is critical because it develops the caramel, butterscotch flavor—but be careful, the mixture may splatter as it boils.)

Remove from heat and stir in butter, vanilla, and butter extract, if using. Divide among four small dessert cups and chill for 2 hours. Makes 1 1/3 -1 1/2 cups.

Preparation = 30 minutes. Serves 4 (makes very small 1/3 cup servings).

								Exchanges		
Calories	Fat	% Fat Cal	Protein	Carbohydrate	Cholesterol	Sodium	Fiber	Carbohydrate	Meat	Fat
160	4 g	24 %	8 g	23 g	64 mg	273 mg	0 g	1 1/2		3/4

(Omitting egg subtracts 14 calories, 1 protein gram, and 53 cholesterol grams.)

*Sugar Alternative: 1/2 cup maple sugar or dried cane juice in place of 1/2 cup brown sugar

CHOCOLATE PUDDING

(can be made without wheat, gluten, dairy, eggs, or refined sugar - see page 9 about ingredients)

Rich and creamy, this pudding is the ultimate comfort food or perfect for a very elegant dinner.

1/3 cup granulated sugar*	1/8 teaspoon salt
2 tablespoons cornstarch or arrowroot	1 3/4 cups low-fat milk (cow, rice, soy, or nut)
2 tablespoons unsweetened cocoa (not Dutch)	1 ounce dairy-free chocolate
1 teaspoon coffee powder (optional)	1 teaspoon gluten-free vanilla extract

Combine first five ingredients in sauce pan; stir well. Gradually whisk in milk. Bring to a boil over medium heat, whisking constantly. Add chocolate and cook for one minute, stirring constantly. Remove from heat and add vanilla. Chill. Makes 2 cups.

Preparation = 15 minutes. Serves 4.

								Exchanges		
Calories	Fat	% Fat Cal	Protein	Carbohydrate	Cholesterol	Sodium	Fiber	Carbohydrate	Meat	Fat
180	5 g	22 %	4 g	30 g	8 mg	132 mg	1 g	2		1

Sugar Alternative: 1/3 cup dried cane juice or maple sugar or date sugar in place of 1/3 cup granulated sugar

VANILLA CUSTARD

(can be made without wheat, gluten, dairy, or refined sugar - see page 9 about ingredients)

This makes a rich, thick, velvety custard. Eat as a pudding or as a filling for layered cakes.

1 cup milk (cow, rice, soy, or nut)	4 large egg yolks at room temperature
1/2 cup granulated sugar*	2 teaspoons gluten-free vanilla extract
1/4 cup cornstarch or arrowroot	1 tablespoon butter or oleo or cooking oil

In medium-size pan, heat milk to simmering (not boiling) over low-medium heat. Set aside. Meanwhile, in small bowl mix together sugar and cornstarch. In another bowl, beat the egg yolks with an electric mixer until thick and lemon-colored. Slowly add cornstarch mixture to eggs, mixing until smooth. Gradually beat hot milk into egg mixture.

Return mixture to pan and cook for 2 minutes, whisking constantly, over low heat until thickened. Remove from heat. Stir in butter and vanilla extract. Transfer to bowl, cover with plastic wrap touching surface of custard. Chill. Makes about 1 1/4 cups.

Preparation = 15 minutes (excludes chilling time). Serves 4.

								Exchanges		
Calories	Fat	% Fat Cal	Protein	Carbohydrate	Cholesterol	Sodium	Fiber	Carbohydrate	Meat	Fat
245	10 g	37 g	5 g	30 mg	229 mg	67 mg	0 g	2		2

Sugar Alternative: 1/2 cup fructose powder in place of 1/2 cup sugar

VANILLA FROZEN YOGURT WITHOUT EGGS

(can be made without wheat, gluten, eggs, or refined sugar - see page 9 about ingredients)

Ice cream is an American institution, so it's only appropriate that all of us have an opportunity to enjoy its smooth, creamy coolness—even if we can't eat all the conventional ingredients that usually go into ice cream. The yogurt produces a creamy texture. However, if this version is not appropriate for you and you can tolerate eggs, try the version on the next page.

2 cups plain or vanilla yogurt*	1/2 cup honey
2 teaspoons unflavored gelatin powder	3 teaspoons gluten-free vanilla extract
1 3/4 cups milk (cow, rice, soy, or nut)	

Place yogurt in strainer lined with paper coffee filter or cheesecloth. Place strainer over large bowl or measuring cup, cover, and refrigerate for 24 hours.

Sprinkle gelatin over 1/4 cup of milk in small bowl. Let stand, stirring frequently, until gelatin swells—about 10 minutes.

Heat remaining milk and the honey over low heat until honey dissolves. Remove from heat. Cool to room temperature, then stir in gelatin mixture, vanilla extract, and yogurt. You may have to use a whisk to thoroughly blend the ingredients. Chill until mixture reaches 40 degrees.

Pour chilled mixture into canister of ice cream machine and churn until frozen. Serve immediately. May store in freezer up to 2 days. Makes 1 quart. Serves 8 (1/2 cup servings.)

Preparation = 15 minutes assembly of ingredients, 40 minutes chilling and approximately 30 minutes to freeze. (The electric Krupps ice cream machine in which this recipe was tested makes ice cream in 20-30 minutes.)

								Exchanges		
Calories	Fat	% Fat Cal	Protein	Carbohydrate	Cholesterol	Sodium	Fiber	Carbohydrate	Meat	Fat
135	2 g	12 %	5 g	26 g	8 mg	74 mg	0 g	1 3/4		1/2

*Dairy Alternative: Yogurt from goat's milk may be used—if you're not allergic to cow's milk. Soy yogurt may be used, however, it may contain brown rice syrup which celiacs should avoid because it may contain barley malt. Also, soy yogurt will not drain so you can eliminate this step.

VANILLA ICE CREAM WITH EGGS

(can be made without wheat, gluten, dairy, or refined sugar - see page 9 about ingredients)

Did you know that the average American consumes an average of 27.4 pints of ice cream per year? This ice cream recipe is designed for people who don't want to eat dairy products, but can eat eggs. Using all egg yolks will yield a richer color.

1 teaspoon unflavored gelatin powder
4 cups whole milk (cow, rice, soy, or nut)
1/2 cup honey
3 teaspoons gluten-free vanilla extract

4 beaten egg yolks, beaten until very smooth (or 2 whole eggs or equivalent liquid egg substitute. Be sure egg substitutes are gluten-free.)

Combine gelatin with 3 tablespoons of the milk and stir until dissolved. Add gelatin mixture, honey, and remaining milk to small saucepan. Cook over low heat until mixture almost boils. Remove from heat.

Whisk 1/2 cup of the hot mixture into eggs. Add eggs to mixture in saucepan, return saucepan to low-medium heat and cook, stirring, for another two minutes. Do not boil, which may cause mixture to curdle. Remove from heat. Stir in vanilla extract. Chill until mixture reaches 40 degrees.

Pour chilled mixture into canister of ice cream machine and churn until frozen. (The electric Krupps ice cream machine in which this recipe was tested makes ice cream in 20-30 minutes.) Serve immediately. May store in freezer up to 2 days. Makes 1 quart. Serves 8 (1/2 cup servings).

Preparation = 15 minutes assembly of ingredients, 40 minutes chilling and approximately 30 minutes to freeze. (The electric Krupps ice cream machine in which this recipe was tested makes ice cream in 20-30 minutes.)

| | | | | | | | | Exchanges | | |
Calories	Fat	% Fat Cal	Protein	Carbohydrate	Cholesterol	Sodium	Fiber	Carbohydrate	Meat	Fat
175	7 g	34 %	6 g	24 g	123 mg	66 mg	0 g	1 1/2		1 1/2

BUTTERSCOTCH SAUCE

(can be made without wheat, gluten, dairy, eggs, or refined sugar - see page 9 about ingredients)

This sauce has a wonderful, butterscotch flavor that is great on ice cream sundaes.

1 cup brown sugar*
2 tablespoons honey
1/2 cup butter or oleo

1/2 cup whole milk (cow, rice, soy, or nut)
1 1/2 teaspoons gluten-free vanilla extract

Place brown sugar (or dried cane juice), honey, and butter in small saucepan over medium heat. Bring to boil, then simmer gently over very low heat for 5 minutes without stirring. Watch carefully so mixture doesn't burn. Remove from heat and stir in milk and vanilla. Makes about 2 cups.

Preparation = 15 minutes. Serves 16 (1 tablespoon each).

Calories	Fat	% Fat Cal	Protein	Carbohydrate	Cholesterol	Sodium	Fiber	Exchanges Carbohydrate	Meat	Fat
95	6 g	53 %	<1 g	11 g	15 mg	65 mg	0 g	3/4		1 1/4

Butterscotch Fudge Sauce: Add 1 ounce of dairy-free chocolate chips or chocolate pieces to the sauce when you add the vanilla and milk. Stir until smooth.

*Sugar Alternative: 1 cup dried cane juice or maple sugar in place of 1 cup brown sugar

CHOCOLATE FUDGE SAUCE

(can be made without wheat, gluten, dairy, eggs, or refined sugar - see page 9 about ingredients)

This sauce has no redeeming qualities—except that it is fabulous and extremely decadent!

1 cup brown sugar or dried cane juice or
   maple sugar
1/4 cup honey
1/3 cup canola, safflower, or other oil

1/2 cup milk (cow, rice, soy, or nut)
2 teaspoons gluten-free vanilla
1/4 cup dairy-free chocolate chips or pieces

Combine brown sugar (or dried cane juice), honey, and oil in small, heavy pan over medium heat. Bring to boil, then simmer gently over very low heat for 5 minutes without stirring. Remove from heat and stir in milk, vanilla, and chocolate until smooth.

Preparation = 10 minutes. Serves 16 (1 tablespoon each).

Calories	Fat	% Fat Cal	Protein	Carbohydrate	Cholesterol	Sodium	Fiber	Exchanges Carbohydrate	Meat	Fat
110	5 g	45 %	<1 g	15 g	1 g	8 mg	0 mg	1		1

BLUEBERRY SAUCE

(can be made without wheat, gluten, dairy, eggs, or refined sugar - see page 9 about ingredients)

Drizzle this flavorful sauce over vanilla or peach ice cream or on New York cheesecake.

1 cup apple juice (or juice of choice)
2 tablespoons honey or pure maple syrup
1/4 cup cornstarch or arrowroot

1 cup blueberries (fresh or frozen)
1 teaspoon fresh lemon juice
1/2 teaspoon grated lemon peel

Place apple juice and honey in small saucepan, reserving enough apple juice to mix with cornstarch (or arrowroot) in a small bowl, forming paste. Over low-medium heat, whisk paste back into saucepan and continue whisking until mixture thickens and boils.

Remove from heat and stir in blueberries, lemon juice, and lemon peel. Serve warm or chilled.

Preparation = 10 minutes. Serves 8 (1/4 cup per serving).

Calories	Fat	% Fat Cal	Protein	Carbohydrate	Cholesterol	Sodium	Fiber	Exchanges Carbohydrate	Meat	Fat
55	0 g	2 %	<1 g	14 g	0 mg	3 mg	<1 g	1		

CINNAMON SAUCE

(can be made without wheat, gluten, dairy, eggs, or refined sugar - see page 9 about ingredients)

This aromatic sauce is great over ice cream, but can also be used on apple pies, cobblers, or other kinds of fruit desserts. It is best when served warm.

1/2 cup brown sugar or dried cane juice
    or 1/4 cup honey
1 tablespoon cornstarch
1/8 teaspoon salt
1 cup water
3/4 teaspoon ground cinnamon

2 tablespoons butter or oleo or canola, safflower, or other oil
1/2 teaspoon grated lemon peel
1 teaspoon lemon juice

In small saucepan over medium-high heat, combine sugar (or honey), cornstarch, and salt. Stir in water and bring to boil, stirring constantly. Reduce heat to low-medium and gently boil sauce until thickened.

Remove from heat and add cinnamon, butter, lemon peel, and lemon juice, stirring until butter is melted and sauce is smooth. Makes 1 1/4 cups.

Preparation = 10 minutes. Serves 6 (<1/4 cup each).

Calories	Fat	% Fat Cal	Protein	Carbohydrate	Cholesterol	Sodium	Fiber	Exchanges Carbohydrate	Meat	Fat
85	4 g	39 %	<1 g	13 g	10 mg	89 mg	0 g	1		3/4

APPETIZERS & SNACKS

Mom. I'm hungry. What can I eat? — Everybody's children

Deciding what should go into this chapter was difficult. Eventually, I settled on a small set of recipes for snacks that are most problematic for people on special diets. That is, these recipes would ordinarily include wheat, gluten, dairy or eggs. But, now you can eat these dishes knowing they're safe for your diet.

See page 9 for more information on the ingredients used in these recipes.

PARTY MIX

(can be made without wheat, gluten, dairy, eggs, or refined sugar - see page 9 about ingredients)

Use the pretzels on the next page to make this party mix complete. You can vary the cereals as you wish, depending on your taste preferences and the availability of various brands in your area. Look for "pure" cereals such as puffed corn that contains no other ingredients but corn.

1 recipe Pretzels (stick shapes -see page 118)
4 cups puffed corn, corn chips or cereal of choice (use several different kinds)
1 cup pecans or walnuts
1 cup almonds, pumpkin seeds or Chickpea "Nuts" (See page 119) – or a mixture of all three
1/2 cup sunflower seeds

1/4 cup melted butter or oleo or use cooking oil (or spray with cooking spray)
1/2 teaspoon garlic powder or onion powder or fresh minced garlic or fresh grated onion
2 teaspoons Italian herb seasoning
1 tablespoon wheat-free soy sauce
1/2 cup Parmesan cheese (cow, rice, or soy – may omit, if desired, with loss of flavor)
1 teaspoon paprika

Combine pretzels, cereals, and nuts in large bowl. Melt butter and add to cereal mixture, stirring until thoroughly coated. Combine onion or garlic powder, Italian herb seasoning, soy sauce, Parmesan cheese, and paprika and toss until thoroughly mixed. Then sprinkle over cereal mixture until thoroughly coated. Spread mixture on baking sheet.

Bake at 275 degrees for 45-50 minutes or until mixture is lightly browned. Stir occasionally. Store in airtight container.

Preparation = 1 hour (excludes preparation of Pretzels). Serves 16 (1/2 cup each).

Calories	Fat	% Fat Cal	Protein	Carbohydrate	Cholesterol	Sodium	Fiber	Exchanges Carbohydrate	Meat	Fat
195	15 g	71 %	6 g	10 g	10 mg	110 mg	3 g	3/4		3

(Using Chickpea nuts in place of all nuts and cooking spray in place of butter subtracts 150 calories, 15 fat grams, and 8 cholesterol grams per serving.)

Variations: For a different taste sensation, replace soy sauce with gluten-free Worcestershire sauce and Italian herb seasoning with your favorite herb mix, or gluten-free seasoned salt. You may use other cereals beside puffed corn, depending on your individual food sensitivities.

PRETZELS

(can be made without wheat, gluten, dairy, eggs, or refined sugar - see page 9 about ingredients)

Pretzels make great snacks. Try dipping them in melted, dairy-free chocolate. Yum!

1 tablespoon gluten-free dry yeast
1/2 cup brown rice flour
1/2 cup tapioca flour
1 tablespoon dry milk powder or non-dairy milk powder
2 teaspoons xanthan gum
1/2 teaspoon salt
1 teaspoon onion powder
1 teaspoon unflavored gelatin powder

2/3 cup warm water (105°)
1/2 teaspoon sugar or honey
1 tablespoon olive oil
1 teaspoon cider vinegar or Ener-G yeast-free/gluten-free vinegar (reconstituted)
1 large egg white, beaten to a foam*
1 tablespoon coarse salt (optional)
cooking spray

In medium mixer bowl, blend the yeast, flours, dry milk powder, xanthan gum, salt, onion powder, and gelatin on low speed. Add warm water, sugar, olive oil, and vinegar. Beat on high speed for 3 minutes. Batter will be consistency of soft cookie dough.

Place dough in large, *heavy-duty* plastic freezer bag that has a 1/4-inch opening cut on one corner. Squeeze dough through opening onto baking sheet that has been coated with cooking spray. You may make traditional pretzel shapes, but straight 3-inch sticks are easier. It works best to hold the bag upright as you squeeze the dough out. Brush lightly with beaten egg white (or egg alternative suggested below). Place pretzels in warm place to rise for 10-15 minutes or until pretzels reach desired size.

Preheat oven to 400 degrees. Sprinkle pretzels with coarse salt. Bake until pretzels are dry and golden brown, about 15 minutes.

Preparation = 1 1/4 hours. Makes about 2 1/2 dozen pretzels.

Per pretzel: Exchanges

Calories	Fat	% Fat Cal	Protein	Carbohydrate	Cholesterol	Sodium	Fiber	Carbohydrate	Meat	Fat
30	<1 g	15%	<1 g	6 g	0 mg	228 mg	<1 g	1/2		

*Egg Alternative: You may omit brushing with egg white, but the pretzels will not have a glossy sheen. Instead, coat pretzels with cooking spray. Olive oil spray yields the "brownest" sheen, but you may use the gluten-free spray of your choice.

Suggestions: For *wider, softer pretzels* cut the opening 1/2-inch wide and remove pretzels from oven when lightly browned, not darkly browned. (Optional: after first rising, immerse pretzels in 2 inches of simmering water with 1 tablespoon baking soda for 30 seconds, then return to baking sheet and bake as directed.) Store in airtight containers to retain softness. For *crispy pretzels*, cut the opening 1/4-inch wide and bake until darkly browned. Turn off oven, open door, and leave pretzels another 10 minutes or until they reach desired crispness.

CHICKPEA "NUTS"

(can be made without wheat, gluten, dairy, eggs, or refined sugar - see page 9 about ingredients)

This appetizer makes a tasty substitute for peanuts—with only 10% of the fat! They're great by themselves or use in the Party Mix (page 117).

16 ounce can of chickpeas or garbanzo beans   1 teaspoon olive oil

Drain and rinse chickpeas. Toss with olive oil. Spread on nonstick baking sheet and bake at 350 degrees for 1 hour. Shake pan several times during cooking for even browning. Use immediately.

Preparation = 1 hour. Serves 6 (about 1/4 cup each).

| | | | | | | | | Exchanges | | |
Calories	Fat	% Fat Cal	Protein	Carbohydrate	Cholesterol	Sodium	Fiber	Carbohydrate	Meat	Fat
95	2 g	15%	4 g	17 g	0 mg	226 mg	3 g	1		1/2

CRACKERS

(can be made without wheat, gluten, dairy, eggs, or refined sugar - see page 9 about ingredients)

These crackers are so easy to make and you can add herbs or spices to suit your own taste.

1/4 cup bean flour* (from Authentic Foods)
1/4 cup potato starch
1/4 cup sweet rice flour
1/2 teaspoon xanthan gum
1/4 teaspoon baking soda
1/2 teaspoon salt
1/2 teaspoon onion powder
2 tablespoons Parmesan cheese (cow, rice, or soy)

2 tablespoons soft butter or canola oil spread (Spectrum™) or oleo
1 tablespoon honey or pure maple syrup
3 tablespoons toasted sesame seeds
2 tablespoons milk (cow, rice, soy, or nut)
1 teaspoon gluten-free cider vinegar
cooking spray

Preheat oven to 350 degrees. Spray a baking sheet with cooking spray.

In a medium mixing bowl, combine the flours, xanthan gum, baking soda, salt, onion powder, and Parmesan cheese. Add the butter and honey and mix until the dough resembles coarse crumbs. Stir in sesame seeds. Add the milk and vinegar. Shape dough into soft ball.

Shape the dough into 20 balls, each 1-inch in diameter, and place on baking sheet at least 2 inches apart. Using the bottom of a drinking glass or a rolling pin, flatten the balls to approximately 1/8-inch thick. Use your fingers to smooth edges of circle.

Bake for 12-15 minutes, or until crackers look firm and slightly toasted. Turn each cracker and bake another 5-7 minutes or until golden brown. (You may sprinkle with additional sesame seeds and salt, if desired.)

Preparation = 30 minutes. Makes about 20 crackers.

Per Cracker:

Calories	Fat	% Fat Cal	Protein	Carbohydrate	Cholesterol	Sodium	Fiber	Carbohydrate	Meat	Fat
45	2 g	42 g	1 g	6 g	4 mg	93 mg	<1 g	1/2		1/2

Exchanges shown in last three columns (Carbohydrate, Meat, Fat).

*Flour Alternative: 1/4 cup brown rice flour in place of 1/4 cup bean flour

CHIP DIP

(can be made without wheat, gluten, dairy, eggs, or refined sugar - see page 9 about ingredients)

This dip is fantastically easy—and tastes creamy and smooth, even though you can make it without dairy products. Avoid the feta cheese if you can't tolerate goat's milk. For a totally dairy-free dip, use 2 cups soft silken tofu in place of the cream cheese and feta cheese. Great with chips or crackers or for dipping vegetables.

8 ounces cream cheese or soy cream cheese (room temperature) or soft silken tofu by Mori-Nu®

4 ounces crumbled feta cheese or use 1/2 cup soft silken tofu by Mori-Nu®)

2 tablespoons milk (cow, rice, soy, or nut) or water

2 teaspoons or more herb of choice (or herb mixture such as Italian herb seasoning)

1 or 2 garlic cloves (or to taste)

1/2 teaspoon cracked black pepper

Garnish with chopped green onion, black olives, tomatoes, chives, etc.

Process all ingredients together in a food processor until very smooth. (Add more milk or water, 1 tablespoon at a time, if mixture is too stiff.) Garnish as desired. Serve with crackers, chips, or vegetables. Makes 1 1/2 cups.

Preparation = 10 minutes. Serves 12 (2 tablespoons each).

								Exchanges		
Calories	Fat	% Fat Cal	Protein	Carbohydrate	Cholesterol	Sodium	Fiber	Carbohydrate	Meat	Fat
60	6 g	80 %	2 g	1 g	19 mg	83 mg	<1 g			1 1/4

Without garnishes

(Using all tofu subtracts 45 calories, 7 fat grams, and 200 cholesterol grams per serving. Using tofu in place of cream cheese only subtracts 40 calories, 6 fat grams, and 25 cholesterol grams per serving.)

SALAD DRESSINGS & SAUCES

Variety is the spice of life. — Unknown

The sauces on our food or the salad dressings on our salads can be a problem for special diets. But, it's easy to make your own versions following these easy recipes. They'll taste great and look just like their original versions—and you'll know they're safe for your diet.

You'll notice that some salad dressings contain a yeast-free/gluten-free vinegar made from a powder by Ener-G. See the Glossary of Ingredients on page 9 for more information.

Salad Dressings

Sauces

See page 9 for information on the special ingredients used in these recipes.

AVOCADO DRESSING

(can be made without wheat, gluten, dairy, eggs, yeast, or refined sugar - see page 9 about ingredients)

This dressing goes especially well with Southwestern dishes.

1 large ripe peeled avocado, mashed
1/3 cup water or chicken broth
1 teaspoon fresh lime juice
1/8 teaspoon grated lime peel
1 garlic clove, minced

1/4 teaspoon dried oregano
1/8 teaspoon ground cumin
1/4 teaspoon onion powder
1/8 teaspoon salt
1/8 teaspoon white pepper

Combine mashed avocado with water and remaining ingredients in food processor or blender. Puree mixture to desired consistency. This dressing is best if served immediately or it darkens. Makes about 1 cup.

Preparation = 5 minutes. Serves 16 (1 tablespoon each).

Calories	Fat	% Fat Cal	Protein	Carbohydrate	Cholesterol	Sodium	Fiber	Exchanges Carbohydrate	Meat	Fat
15	1	77%	>1 g	<1 g	0 mg	21 mg	<1 g			1/4

BALSAMIC VINEGAR DRESSING

(can be made without wheat, gluten, dairy, eggs, or refined sugar - see page 9 about ingredients)

If you can tolerate fermented ingredients, balsamic vinegar is an excellent way to add loads of flavor to your salads. True balsamic vinegar, which should be labeled "Aceto Balsamico Tradizionale de Modena", is made from the sweet juice of white grapes. It is not grain-based.

1/2 cup balsamic vinegar
2 tablespoons honey

1/2 teaspoon salt
1 cup extra-virgin olive oil

Place first 3 ingredients in a blender and process until blended. With blender on high, add oil in a steady stream and process until smooth. Refrigerate in airtight container. Makes 1 1/4 cups.

Preparation = 10 minutes. Serves 20 (1 tablespoon each).

Calories	Fat	% Fat Cal	Protein	Carbohydrate	Cholesterol	Sodium	Fiber	Exchanges Carbohydrate	Meat	Fat
105	10 g	90 %	0 mg	3 g	0 mg	53 mg	0 g	1/4		2

CITRUS DRESSING

(can be made without wheat, gluten, dairy, eggs, yeast, or refined sugar - see page 9 about ingredients)

The citrus base of this dressing, accented by fennel and basil, is refreshing.

2 tablespoons fresh lemon juice
1/4 cup fresh orange juice
2 teaspoons fresh lime juice
2 tablespoons olive oil
1 tablespoon grated orange peel
2 teaspoons grated lime peel

1/4 teaspoon crushed red pepper
2 teaspoons fennel seed
2 teaspoons dried basil
1/8 teaspoon salt
dash of white pepper

Combine all ingredients in blender and process until well blended. Refrigerate in airtight container for up to 1 week. Makes about 1/2 cup.

Preparation = 10 minutes. Serves 8 (1 tablespoon each).

Calories	Fat	% Fat Cal	Protein	Carbohydrate	Cholesterol	Sodium	Fiber	Exchanges Carbohydrate	Meat	Fat
35	4 g	80%	0 g	1 g	0 mg	89 mg	0 g			3/4

FRENCH DRESSING

(can be made without wheat, gluten, dairy, eggs, yeast, or refined sugar - see page 9 about ingredients)

This is an all American favorite.

2 tablespoons cider vinegar or Ener-G yeast-free/ gluten-free vinegar (reconstituted)
2 tablespoons fresh lemon juice
2 teaspoons sugar or 1 teaspoon honey
1/2 teaspoon salt
1/4 teaspoon white pepper

1/2 teaspoon dry mustard
1/2 teaspoon paprika
dash cayenne pepper
1/3 cup canola, safflower, or other oil
2 tablespoons water

Place all ingredients, except oil, in blender and process until smooth. With motor running, add oil and process until smooth. Refrigerate in airtight container. Shake just before serving. Makes about 3/4 cup.

Preparation = 10 minutes. Serves 6 (2 tablespoons each).

Calories	Fat	% Fat Cal	Protein	Carbohydrate	Cholesterol	Sodium	Fiber	Exchanges Carbohydrate	Meat	Fat
60	6 g	92 %	0 g	1 mg	0 mg	89 mg	0 g			1 1/4

ITALIAN DRESSING

(can be made without wheat, gluten, dairy, eggs, or refined sugar - see page 9 about ingredients)

Italian dressing is very versatile. Use on salad greens but also as a marinade for meats or fish.

1/2 cup cider vinegar or Ener-G yeast-free/gluten-free vinegar (reconstituted)
1/4 teaspoon oregano leaves
1/2 teaspoon freeze-dried chives
1/2 teaspoon dried parsley flakes
1/4 teaspoon dry mustard
1/8 teaspoon white pepper
1/8 teaspoon garlic powder or fresh garlic

1/4 teaspoon dried chervil (optional)
1/2 teaspoon salt
1/2 teaspoon Parmesan cheese (cow, rice, or soy)
1 tablespoon chopped onion
1/2 teaspoon honey
dash cayenne pepper
1/2 cup extra-virgin olive oil
1/2 cup water or chicken broth

Combine all ingredients in blender and blend well. Refrigerate in airtight container. Makes 1 1/2 cups.

Preparation = 10 minutes. Serves 24 (1 tablespoon each).

Calories	Fat	% Fat Cal	Protein	Carbohydrate	Cholesterol	Sodium	Fiber	Exchanges Carbohydrate	Meat	Fat
40	5 g	96 %	0 g	<1 g	0 mg	45 mg	<1 g			1

LEMON VINAIGRETTE

(can be made without wheat, gluten, dairy, eggs, or refined sugar - see page 9 about ingredients)

Use this flavorful dressing on a seafood salad or on greens. Vary the herbs to suit your taste. You may use 2 teaspoons dry mustard in place of the Dijonnaise.

1 garlic clove, minced (or more to taste)
1/2 cup fresh lemon juice
1 tablespoon honey
2 tablespoons extra-virgin olive oil
1 tablespoon Dijonnaise (gluten-free mustard)
1/2 teaspoon fennel seeds (crushed)

1/8 teaspoon crushed red pepper
1 teaspoon dried parsley or 1 tablespoon fresh parsley, chopped
1/2 teaspoon salt
1 teaspoon dried oregano
dash of white pepper

Place all ingredients in blender and process until smooth. Refrigerate in airtight container. Shake before serving. Makes 1 cup.

Preparation = 10 minutes. Serves 16 (1 tablespoon each).

Calories	Fat	% Fat Cal	Protein	Carbohydrate	Cholesterol	Sodium	Fiber	Exchanges Carbohydrate	Meat	Fat
20	2 g	65 %	<1 g	2 g	0 mg	80 mg	<1 g			1/2

LIME CILANTRO DRESSING

(can be made without wheat, gluten, dairy, eggs, yeast, or refined sugar - see page 9 about ingredients)

This is a perfect dressing for a salad served with a Southwestern meal.

1 teaspoon grated lime peel	1 medium garlic clove
1/4 cup fresh lime juice	1/2 teaspoon honey
1/4 cup fresh lemon juice	1/2 cup extra-virgin olive oil
1/4 cup fresh cilantro, chopped	1/4 cup water
1/2 teaspoon salt	1/8 teaspoon cumin powder

Combine all ingredients in blender and process until completely mixed. Refrigerate in airtight container for up to 1 week. Makes about 1 cup.

Preparation = 10 minutes. Serves 16 (1 tablespoon each).

| | | | | | | | | Exchanges | | |
Calories	Fat	% Fat Cal	Protein	Carbohydrate	Cholesterol	Sodium	Fiber	Carbohydrate	Meat	Fat
65	7 g	94 %	0 g	<1 g	0 mg	67 mg	<1 g			1/2

ORIENTAL DRESSING

(can be made without wheat, gluten, dairy, eggs, yeast, or refined sugar - see page 9 about ingredients)

This makes a nice, light salad dressing to serve with fish or chicken entrees.

1 garlic clove	1/2 cup rice vinegar or Ener-G yeast-
2 tablespoons brown sugar or pure maple syrup	free/gluten-free vinegar (reconstituted)
6 mint leaves (1 teaspoon dried mint)	1/4 cup olive oil
2 thin slices ginger root	dash cayenne pepper
2 tablespoons lime or lemon juice	dash salt & pepper

Place all ingredients in a blender and blend until thoroughly mixed. Store in airtight container in refrigerator. Makes approximately 1 cup.

Preparation = 10 minutes. Serves 16 (1 tablespoon each).

| | | | | | | | | Exchanges | | |
Calories	Fat	% Fat Cal	Protein	Carbohydrate	Cholesterol	Sodium	Fiber	Carbohydrate	Meat	Fat
45	4 g	68 %	<1 g	49 g	0 mg	2 mg	<1 g	3 1/4		3/4

RANCH DRESSING

(can be made without wheat, gluten, eggs, dairy, yeast, or refined sugar - see page 9 about ingredients)

This perennial favorite is great on a salad, but can top baked potatoes or be the basis for a dip.

1/2 cup gluten-free mayonnaise or Egg-Free Mayonnaise (See page 145)
1/2 cup (cow, rice, soy, or nut)
1/4 teaspoon onion salt
1/8 teaspoon garlic salt
1/4 teaspoon black pepper

1/4 teaspoon dried marjoram
1/4 teaspoon celery salt
1/4 teaspoon dried marjoram
dash dried savory leaves (optional)
1/4 teaspoon dried parsley flakes

Combine ingredients in blender and process until blended. Refrigerate in airtight container for one week. Makes 1 cup.

Preparation = 10 minutes. Serves 16 (1 tablespoon each).

| | | | | | | | | Exchanges | | |
Calories	Fat	% Fat Cal	Protein	Carbohydrate	Cholesterol	Sodium	Fiber	Carbohydrate	Meat	Fat
55	5 g	93 %	<1 g	<1 g	5 mg	56 mg	0 g			1

SESAME DRESSING

(can be made without wheat, gluten, dairy, eggs, or refined sugar - see page 9 about ingredients)

This dressing is especially tasty when served with fish, chicken, or Asian main dishes.

1/4 cup canola, safflower, or other oil
1/4 cup sesame oil
1/2 cup rice vinegar or Ener-G yeast-free/gluten-free vinegar (reconstituted)
2 teaspoons salt
2 teaspoons honey

2 tablespoons grated orange rind
1 teaspoon black pepper
1 teaspoon minced fresh ginger root
1 teaspoon wheat-free soy sauce
1 small garlic clove, minced
1/4 teaspoon dried crushed red pepper

Blend all ingredients in blender until smooth. Refrigerate in airtight container. Shake before serving. Makes 1 cup.

Preparation = 10 minutes. Serves 16 (1 tablespoon each).

| | | | | | | | | Exchanges | | |
Calories	Fat	% Fat Cal	Protein	Carbohydrate	Cholesterol	Sodium	Fiber	Carbohydrate	Meat	Fat
65	7 g	91 %	<1 g	2 g	0 mg	284 mg	<1 g			1 1/2

SOY DRESSING

(can be made without wheat, gluten, dairy, eggs, or refined sugar - see page 9 about ingredients)

This dressing complements Asian flavors, so serve it on greens accompanying Asian entrees.

2 tablespoons wheat-free soy sauce
1 tablespoon rice vinegar or Ener-G yeast-free/gluten-free vinegar (reconstituted)
juice of 1 lime
1 teaspoon honey

1 serrano chile, seeded and chopped fine
1/4 teaspoon each salt and pepper
2 tablespoons canola, safflower, or other o
1 tablespoon chopped cilantro (optional)
1 teaspoon sesame oil

Place all ingredients in blender and process until smooth. Refrigerate in airtight container. Makes about 1/2 cup. (Wear gloves while cutting serrano chile.)

Preparation = 10 minutes. Serves 8 (1 tablespoon each).

| | | | | | | | | Exchanges | | |
Calories	Fat	% Fat Cal	Protein	Carbohydrate	Cholesterol	Sodium	Fiber	Carbohydrate	Meat	Fat
45	4 g	79 %	<1g	2 g	0 mg	274 mg	<1 g			3/4

THOUSAND ISLAND DRESSING

(can be made without wheat, gluten, dairy, eggs, or refined sugar - see page 9 about ingredients)

This is the dressing most often used in Reuben sandwiches, which can be made using the Pumpernickel recipe in this book.

1 cup gluten-free mayonnaise or Egg-Free Mayonnaise (See page 145)
3 tablespoons Chili Sauce (See page 131)
1 tablespoon chopped green pepper

1 teaspoon chopped canned pimientos (option
1 teaspoon chopped chives (freeze-dried) or 1 tablespoon fresh chopped chives

Blend ingredients thoroughly in blender. Refrigerate in airtight container. Makes 1 1/4 cups.

Preparation = 10 minutes. Serves 20 (1 tablespoon each).

| | | | | | | | | Exchanges | | |
Calories	Fat	% Fat Cal	Protein	Carbohydrate	Cholesterol	Sodium	Fiber	Carbohydrate	Meat	Fat
80	9 g	96 %	0 g	<1 g	6 mg	67 mg	0 g			2

BARBECUE SAUCE

(can be made without wheat, gluten, dairy, eggs, or refined sugar - see page 9 about ingredients)

I've been making this sauce for more than 20 years and it remains a family favorite. A rich, thick, barbecue sauce, it's wonderful on beef or pork, but I've also used it on chicken, too.

1 cup gluten-free Ketchup (See page 144)
1/2 cup molasses
2 tablespoons dried minced onion or 1 tablespoon grated fresh onion
2 tablespoons brown sugar or honey
1 tablespoon mustard seed
1 teaspoon crushed red pepper
1 teaspoon dried oregano
1/2 teaspoon black pepper

2 teaspoons paprika
1 teaspoon chili powder
1/2 teaspoon salt
1 bay leaf
1 garlic clove, minced
1/2 cup fresh orange juice
1/4 cup olive oil
1/4 cup cider vinegar or Ener-G yeast-free/gluten-free vinegar (reconstituted)

Combine all ingredients in small saucepan. Bring to boil over medium heat. Reduce heat and simmer gently for 20 minutes. Remove bay leaf. Makes 2 cups.

Preparation = 20 minutes. Serves 8 (1/4 cup each).

								Exchanges		
Calories	Fat	% Fat Cal	Protein	Carbohydrate	Cholesterol	Sodium	Fiber	Carbohydrate	Meat	Fat
180	8 g	35%	1 g	30 g	0 mg	54 mg	1 g	2		1 1/2

CHILI SAUCE

(can be made without wheat, gluten, dairy, eggs, yeast, or refined sugar - see page 9 about ingredients)

Use this sauce on meats or in Thousand Island Dressing (See page 130).

6 large ripe tomatoes (peeled, chopped)
2 large onions, finely chopped
2 large green peppers, finely chopped
1/2 cup cider vinegar or Ener-G yeast-free/gluten-free vinegar (reconstituted)
3/4 teaspoon salt
1/4 teaspoon cinnamon

1/4 teaspoon ground cloves
1/4 teaspoon ginger
1 teaspoon celery seed
1/4 teaspoon crushed red pepper
1/4 teaspoon dry mustard
3/4 cup granulated sugar or 1/3 cup honey

Combine all ingredients in large pan over low-medium heat. Simmer gently, uncovered, for 45-60 minutes, or until thickened. Stir frequently to prevent sticking. Remove from heat and cool slightly. Refrigerate in airtight container. Makes about 3 cups.
Preparation = 1 1/4 hour. Serves 24 (2 tablespoons each.)

								Exchanges		
Calories	Fat	% Fat Cal	Protein	Carbohydrate	Cholesterol	Sodium	Fiber	Carbohydrate	Meat	Fat
35	<1 g	3 g	<1 g	8 g	0 mg	115 mg	<1 g	1/2		

HOLLANDAISE SAUCE

(can be made without wheat, gluten, dairy, or refined sugar - see page 9 about ingredients)

The traditional Hollandaise Sauce is loaded with fat, calories—and wheat and dairy. This revised version lowers the fat and calories dramatically. I think you'll agree—this is a winner! Use it for the Eggs Benedict on page 71.

2 **large egg yolks**
1 **cup Yogurt Cheese (See page 142) or 1 cup**
    soft silken tofu by Mori-Nu®
3 **tablespoons fresh lemon juice**
1/2 **teaspoon xanthan gum**
2 **tablespoons butter or oleo or other cooking oil**

1/4 **teaspoon salt**
1/8 **teaspoon cayenne pepper**
1/8 **teaspoon white pepper**
1/4 **teaspoon dry mustard**

Blend egg yolks, Yogurt Cheese (or tofu), lemon juice, and xanthan gum in blender until light and fluffy. Place the egg yolk mixture in the top of a double boiler set over simmering, not boiling, water. (Don't let bottom of double boiler touch the water.) Add butter (or oil), whisking constantly until mixture thickens. If too thick, add 1 tablespoon hot water.

Remove from heat and stir in salt, cayenne pepper, white pepper, and dry mustard. (Mixture can be kept warm over simmering water for about 30 minutes. If it starts to separate, add a teaspoon of boiling water and whisk briskly until smooth.) Makes 1 cup.

Preparation = 15 minutes. Serves 4 (1/4 cup each).

Calories	Fat	% Fat Cal	Protein	Carbohydrate	Cholesterol	Sodium	Fiber	Exchanges Carbohydrate	Meat	Fat
115	8 g	65 %	5 g	6 g	123 mg	240 mg	0 g	1/2		1 1/2

(Using tofu adds 11 calories and 3 fat grams, but subtracts 3 carbohydrate grams, 17 cholesterol grams and 100 sodium grams.)

LEMON-TOMATO BARBECUE SAUCE

(can be made without wheat, gluten, dairy, eggs, or refined sugar - see page 9 about ingredients)

A very light, low-fat sauce that is especially good on grilled chicken. I've been making this sauce for 25 years and my guests always ask for the recipe.

1 can tomato juice (5.5-ounces)	1 teaspoon gluten-free Worcestershire
1 small garlic clove, minced	Sauce (See page 147) or use wheat-free
1/2 teaspoon onion powder	soy sauce
1/4 teaspoon lemon pepper	1/4 cup fresh lemon juice
1/8 teaspoon cayenne pepper	1 tablespoon butter or oleo or cooking oil

Place all ingredients in a small, heavy saucepan. Bring to boil over medium heat, reduce heat to low, and simmer for 5 minutes. Baste chicken as it cooks on the grill. Makes about 3/4 cup.

Preparation = 10 minutes. Serves 6 (about 3 tablespoons each).

								Exchanges		
Calories	Fat	% Fat Cal	Protein	Carbohydrate	Cholesterol	Sodium	Fiber	Carbohydrate	Meat	Fat
25	2 g	60 %	0 g	3 g	5 mg	137 mg	0 g			1/2

PIZZA SAUCE

(can be made without wheat, gluten, dairy, eggs, or refined sugar - see page 9 about ingredients)

Prepare this fat-free sauce while the Pizza Crust bakes. It fills the kitchen with a delicious, intoxicating aroma. And, by letting it simmer for 15 minutes, it becomes thick so it won't make the pizza crust soggy. You may omit the sugar, if you wish.

8 ounces gluten-free tomato sauce (or
   make your own with recipe on page 146)
1/2 teaspoon dried oregano
1/2 teaspoon dried basil
1/2 teaspoon dried rosemary

1/2 teaspoon fennel seeds
1/4 teaspoon garlic powder
2 teaspoons sugar or 1 teaspoon honey
1/2 teaspoon salt

Combine all ingredients in small saucepan and bring to boil over medium heat. Reduce heat to low and simmer for 15 minutes, while Pizza Crust is being assembled.

Top Pizza Crust with sauce and your preferred toppings. Makes about 1 cup.

Preparation = 15 minutes. Serves 4 (about 1/4 cup each).

Calories	Fat	% Fat Cal	Protein	Carbohydrate	Cholesterol	Sodium	Fiber	Exchanges Carbohydrate	Meat	Fat
120	<1 g	5 %	4 g	27 g	0 mg	557 mg	3 g	1 3/4		

PESTO

(can be made without wheat, gluten, dairy, eggs, or refined sugar - see page 9 about ingredients)

Use this tasty pesto sauce on pasta, pizza, or tossed with vegetables.

2 cups fresh basil leaves, tightly packed
1-3 peeled garlic cloves
3 tablespoons pine nuts (optional)
2 tablespoons olive oil

1/4 cup Parmesan cheese (cow, rice, or soy)
 or omit cheese, if desired
3/4 teaspoon salt

Puree all ingredients in food processor until smooth. If not using immediately, refrigerate in tightly covered glass jar. Makes 1 cup.

Preparation = 10 minutes. Serves 4 (about 1/4 cup each).

Calories	Fat	% Fat Cal	Protein	Carbohydrate	Cholesterol	Sodium	Fiber	Exchanges Carbohydrate	Meat	Fat
105	8 g	64 %	6 g	4 g	4 mg	496 mg	<1 g	1/4		1 1/2

SPICY PESTO

(can be made without wheat, gluten, dairy, eggs, yeast, or refined sugar - see page 9 about ingredients)

This pesto is especially flavorful and can be tossed with your favorite gluten-free pasta. Or simply top a broiled fish fillet or chicken breast for instant flavor.

2 tablespoons chopped fresh cilantro
1 tablespoon chopped fresh parsley
1 teaspoon dried basil
1 teaspoon dried mint
1 teaspoon ground cumin
1 teaspoon ground allspice
1/8 teaspoon cayenne pepper

1 medium garlic clove, crushed
2 green onions, chopped
1 tablespoon cider vinegar or Ener-G yeast-
 free/gluten-free vinegar (reconstituted)
1 tablespoon fresh lemon juice
1/4 cup olive oil
1/2 teaspoon freshly ground black pepper

Place all ingredients in food processor and process until mixture reaches desired consistency. Refrigerate in airtight container for up to 1 week. Use on pasta, risotto, or vegetables—or add to soups, stews or sauces for a quick flavor boost. Makes 1/2 cup.

Preparation = 15 minutes. Serves 8 (1 tablespoon each).

Calories	Fat	% Fat Cal	Protein	Carbohydrate	Cholesterol	Sodium	Fiber	Exchanges Carbohydrate	Meat	Fat
75	7 g	78 %	1 g	4 g	0 mg	7 mg	1 g			1 1/2

SPAGHETTI SAUCE

(can be made without wheat, gluten, dairy, eggs, or refined sugar - see page 9 about ingredients)

I've been making this low-fat sauce for nearly 25 years and, even though we've tried several others, it remains our favorite. The crock pot works best. However, you can simmer it on the stove if you wish—adding additional water if mixture becomes too thick.

1 large can low-sodium tomato juice (48 ounces)
3 cans gluten-free tomato paste (6 ounces each)
3 tablespoons dried parsley
2 tablespoons dried basil
1 tablespoon dried rosemary
2 bay leaves
2 teaspoons oregano

1 teaspoon black pepper
3 tablespoons sugar or 1 1/2 table spoons honey
2 teaspoons salt
1/4 cup Romano or Parmesan cheese (cheese may be omitted)

In large crock pot, combine all ingredients. Mix well. Cook all day on low-medium heat. Or cook in large pot on stovetop all day. Stir occasionally. Makes about 8 cups of sauce.

Preparation = 6-8 hours in crock pot; 2-3 hours on stovetop. Serves 16 (1/2 cup each).

| | | | | | | | | | Exchanges | | |
Calories	Fat	% Fat Cal	Protein	Carbohydrate	Cholesterol	Sodium	Fiber	Carbohydrate	Meat	Fat
60	1 g	12 %	3 g	13 g	2 mg	320 mg	2 g	3/4		1/4

WHITE SAUCE

(can be made without wheat, gluten, dairy, eggs, or refined sugar - see page 9 about ingredients)

Use this easy Bechamel sauce on vegetables or in any meat dish that requires a white sauce.

1 3/4 cups milk (cow, rice, soy, or nut)
1 slice of onion (1/4-inch thick) or 1/4 teaspoon onion powder
1 bay leaf
1/4 teaspoon salt
1/2 teaspoon dried thyme
1/4 teaspoon white pepper
1 tablespoon butter or canola, safflower, or other oil
2 tablespoons cornstarch or arrowroot dissolved in 3 tablespoons water
dash of ground nutmeg

In small saucepan over low-medium heat, bring milk, onion, bay leaf, thyme, white pepper, and oil to simmer. Remove from heat and let stand for 10 minutes to blend the flavors. Strain and discard solids. (Or tie onion, bay leaf, and thyme in a piece of cheesecloth and remove after 10 minutes.)

Return saucepan to medium heat. Stir in cornstarch mixture and continue whisking until mixture thickens. Remove from heat. Add nutmeg. Makes 1 3/4 cups.

Preparation = 15 minutes. Serves 6 (about 1/4 cup each).

| | | | | | | | | Exchanges | | |
Calories	Fat	% Fat Cal	Protein	Carbohydrate	Cholesterol	Sodium	Fiber	Carbohydrate	Meat	Fat
55	4 g	60 %	2 g	4 g	6 g	109 ng	0 g	1/4		3/4

BAKING SUBSTITUTES & CONDIMENTS

Laughter is brightest where food is best. — Irish proverb

Sometimes, it's the simple, little ingredients that cause the most difficulty for people on special diets. This section contains recipes for the condiments we put on our food and the simple baking ingredients we never think about—until our special diets force us to re-examine everything that goes in our mouths.

Baking Substitutes

Condiments

See page 9 for information on the special ingredients used in these recipes.

BAKING POWDER WITH CORN

(can be made without wheat, gluten, dairy, eggs, yeast, or refined sugar)

I prefer to use this version of baking powder when the recipe relies on a large amount of baking powder. The reason is that baking powder used in large amounts can impart a bitterness that interferes with the dish's flavor. If you can't eat corn, try the Baking Powder Without Corn on this page.

1/4 cup cream of tartar　　　　　**2 tablespoons baking soda**
3 tablespoons cornstarch

Combine all ingredients in a jar. Cover tightly and shake vigorously to mix. Store at room temperature up to 1 month. Makes a generous 1/2 cup. Double recipe if you wish.

Preparation = 5 minutes

Per teaspoon:

| | | | | | | | | Exchanges | | |
Calories	Fat	% Fat Cal	Protein	Carbohydrate	Cholesterol	Sodium	Fiber	Carbohydrate	Meat	Fat
10	0 g	0 %	0 g	2 g	0 mg	316 mg	0 g			

BAKING POWDER WITHOUT CORN

(can be made without wheat, gluten, dairy, eggs, yeast, refined sugar, or corn)

When the recipe calls for 1 teaspoon baking powder, you may use 1 1/2 teaspoons of this corn-free version. Make this mix frequently rather than doubling it— it loses potency over time.

3 tablespoons baking soda　　　　　**1/3 cup arrowroot**
1/3 cup cream of tartar

Combine all ingredients in a jar. Cover tightly and shake vigorously to mix. Store at room temperature up to 1 month. Makes about 3/4 cup.

Preparation = 5 minutes

Per teaspoon:

| | | | | | | | | Exchanges | | |
Calories	Fat	% Fat Cal	Protein	Carbohydrate	Cholesterol	Sodium	Fiber	Carbohydrate	Meat	Fat
10	0 g	0 %	0 g	2 g	0 mg	315 mg	0 g			

NUT MILK

(can be made without wheat, gluten, dairy, eggs, or refined sugar - see page 9 about ingredients)

Add 1/4 teaspoon soy lecithin or 1/4 cup banana (or other fruit) for a fuller bodied milk.

1/2 cup chopped cashews or almonds (or other unroasted nuts of your choice)

2 cups warm water (may adjust amount)
1 teaspoon honey and dash vanilla (to taste)

Blend nuts, water, and honey in blender until mixture is very, very smooth. Strain mixture, refrigerate in airtight container for up to 3 days. Makes about 2 cups.

Preparation = 10 minutes. Serves 2 (1 cup each).

Per cup:

Calories	Fat	% Fat Cal	Protein	Carbohydrate	Cholesterol	Sodium	Fiber	Exchanges Carbohydrate	Meat	Fat
195	15 g	67 %	5 g	12 g	0 mg	13 mg	1 g	3/4		3

SOUR CREAM

(can be made without wheat, gluten, dairy, or eggs - see page 9 about ingredients)

Use on baked potatoes or in dips, but may not perform the same way in baking as real sour cream.

10.5 ounces soft silken tofu by Mori-Nu®
2 tablespoons cider vinegar or Ener-G yeast--free/gluten-free vinegar (reconstituted)

1 tablespoon fresh lemon juice
1 teaspoon Butter Buds or butter-flavored salt or gluten-free butter extract

Process all ingredients in food processor or blender until very, very smooth. Refrigerate in airtight container. Makes 1 1/4 cups.

Preparation = 5 minutes. Serves 20 (1 tablespoon each).

Per tablespoon:

Calories	Fat	% Fat Cal	Protein	Carbohydrate	Cholesterol	Sodium	Fiber	Exchanges Carbohydrate	Meat	Fat
10	<1 g	45 %	<1 g	1 g	0 mg	6 mg	0 g			

YOGURT CHEESE

(can be made without wheat, gluten, eggs, or refined sugar - see page 9 about ingredients)

Use this in place of sour cream. Goat yogurt will work, if you're not allergic to milk.

Place 8 ounces plain, lowfat yogurt in strainer lined with cheesecloth or paper coffee filter. Refrigerate, covered, for 24 hours. Discard liquid (whey). Refrigerate for 1 week.

Per tablespoon:

Calories	Fat	% Fat Cal	Protein	Carbohydrate	Cholesterol	Sodium	Fiber	Exchanges Carbohydrate	Meat	Fat
10	0 g	3 %	1 g	1 g	0 mg	11 mg	0 g			

APPLE BUTTER

(can be made without wheat, gluten, dairy, eggs, or refined sugar - see page 9 about ingredients)

Although you can purchase apple butter, making it yourself allows you to control the amount and type of sweetener—without any ingredients you don't want such as corn syrup. It takes awhile to simmer, but if you cook the apples while you cook dinner you're right there to give them an occasional stir as they simmer on the stove. And, your kitchen will smell absolutely heavenly! Use the apple butter on muffins or toast and as a natural sweetener in recipes such as Baked Doughnuts (See pages 49-50) or Zucchini Bread (See page 39).

1 pound tart cooking apples (about 3 Granny Smith), peeled and chopped	1 cup apple juice or water
1 orange	1/8 teaspoon ground cinnamon
1 lemon	1/8 teaspoon ground allspice
2 tablespoons brown sugar or maple sugar or dried cane juice or honey	1/2 teaspoon gluten-free vanilla
	dash salt

Place apples in a large, heavy-bottomed saucepan. Remove a 3-inch long strip of peel from the orange and lemon and add to apples. Squeeze juice from the orange and lemon and add juice to pan. Add remaining ingredients.

Bring mixture to boil, cover, and cook over low heat for 15 minutes. Uncover the pan and continue to cook over very low heat until mixture is very thick—about 45 minutes. The liquid will have evaporated, so you must stir almost continuously during the final 15 minutes of cooking.

Two alternatives after cooking over low heat for 15 minutes: 1) place the mixture in an oven-proof dish and bake at 300 degrees, stirring every 10 minutes or so until liquid is evaporated; 2) place mixture in crock pot and cook all day. Cool mixture to room temperature.

Work the apple butter through a food mill, a sieve, or puree in food processor if you want really smooth butter. Refrigerate in airtight container for up to 1 week. Makes 1 cup.

Preparation = 1 1/4 hours. Serves 16 (1 tablespoon each).

Per tablespoon: Exchanges

Calories	Fat	% Fat Cal	Protein	Carbohydrate	Cholesterol	Sodium	Fiber	Carbohydrate	Meat	Fat
30	<1 g	3 %	<1 g	7 g	0 mg	17 mg	<1 g	1/2		

KETCHUP

(can be made without wheat, gluten, dairy, eggs, or refined sugar - see page 9 about ingredients)

Making your own condiments is not hard at all and assures you of an allergy-free product because you personally select all the ingredients. This ketchup is very easy and very flavorful. Remember, you need to give it an occasional stir every 15 minutes or so.

4 medium onions, chopped
4 garlic cloves, minced
3 28-ounce cans of whole gluten-free tomatoes, drained
1 cup cider vinegar or Ener-G yeast-free/ gluten-free vinegar (reconstituted)
2 cans gluten-free tomato paste
1 teaspoon salt (or to taste)
2 teaspoons dry mustard (Colman's is best)

1/2 teaspoon dried oregano
1/2 teaspoon freshly ground black pepper
1/4 teaspoon cayenne pepper
1 teaspoon paprika
1 teaspoon whole cloves
1 teaspoon whole allspice
1 stick cinnamon
1 teaspoon celery seed
1/4 cup brown sugar*

In large, heavy Dutch oven combine onions, garlic, and drained tomatoes (reserve drained tomato juice for another use). Cover and cook over moderately low heat, stirring occasionally, until onions are very soft, about 30 minutes. Remove from heat and cool for 30 minutes. Puree mixture in blender in small batches until smooth.

Return tomato mixture to Dutch oven and add vinegar. Simmer, uncovered, over low heat until mixture is reduced by half. Stir frequently to avoid scorching.

Stir tomato paste, salt, mustard, oregano, black pepper, cayenne pepper, and paprika into mixture. Tie cloves, allspice, cinnamon, and celery seed in a piece of cheesecloth (or use 1/2 teaspoon dried version of cloves, allspice and cinnamon and just stir into mixture) and add to mixture. Simmer, stirring frequently, until very thick or until reduced to a consistency you like. Discard cheesecloth bag. Add sugar (or sweetener of choice) and stir until completely dissolved. (You may add sweetener earlier in the cooking process, However, the mixture will burn more quickly and will need constant stirring.)

Remove from heat. Cool slightly, then transfer to glass container with tight fitting lid. Refrigerate for up to 2 months. Makes about 4 cups (depending on how long the mixture is cooked).

Preparation = 3-4 hours. Serves 64 (1 tablespoon each).

Per tablespoon: Exchanges

Calories	Fat	% Fat Cal	Protein	Carbohydrate	Cholesterol	Sodium	Fiber	Carbohydrate	Meat	Fat
25	<1 g	8 %	<1 g	4 g	0 mg	132 mg	<1 g	1/4		

*Sugar Alternative #1: 1/4 cup dried cane juice
*Sugar Alternative #2: 1/4 cup maple sugar
*Sugar Alternative #3: 3 tablespoons honey
*Sugar Alternative #4: Use your favorite non-calorie sweetener.

EGG-FREE MAYONNAISE #1

(can be made without wheat, gluten, dairy, eggs, yeast, or refined sugar - see page 9 about ingredients)

Both of these mayonnaise recipes are super-easy. You may omit the sugar, if you wish.

2   teaspoons sweet rice flour
1/4   teaspoon dry mustard
1/4   teaspoon salt
1/4   teaspoon sugar or honey
1/8   teaspoon white pepper
1/8   teaspoon cayenne pepper

dash of paprika
1/4   cup fresh lemon juice
1/4   cup water
1   teaspoon cider vinegar or Ener-G yeast-
   -free/gluten-free vinegar (reconstituted)
1/4   cup canola, safflower, or other oil

Combine flour, mustard, salt, sugar (or honey), peppers, paprika, lemon juice, and water in small, heavy pan. Over low-medium heat, bring to a boil and whisk until mixture is thickened.

Remove from heat and cool for 2-3 minutes. Combine the vinegar and oil and slowly pour into flour mixture, whisking constantly until completely blended. Refrigerate in airtight container for up to 1 week. Makes slightly under 1 cup.

Preparation = 15 minutes. Serves 16 (1 tablespoon each).

Per tablespoon:

Calories	Fat	% Fat Cal	Protein	Carbohydrate	Cholesterol	Sodium	Fiber	Carbohydrate	Meat	Fat
								Exchanges		
35	3 g	91 %	0 g	1 g	0 mg	34 mg	0 g			1/2

EGG-FREE MAYONNAISE #2

(can be made without wheat, gluten, eggs or refined sugar - see page 9 about ingredients)

1   cup plain, low-fat yogurt
1/4   teaspoon dry mustard
1/4   teaspoon grated lemon peel
1/4   teaspoon sugar or honey

1/4   teaspoon salt
1/8   teaspoon cayenne pepper
1/8   teaspoon white pepper

Place the yogurt in a strainer lined with a coffee filter or cheesecloth. Place strainer over bowl, cover the entire thing with a large plastic bag or foil and refrigerate for 24 hours. Discard liquid (whey). (You may use goat yogurt or soy yogurt, if you can tolerate them, but soy yogurt won't drain.)

In small bowl, whisk together the yogurt and remaining ingredients until thoroughly blended. Makes 1 cup.

Preparation = 10 minutes. Serves 16 (1 tablespoon each).

Per tablespoon:

Calories	Fat	% Fat Cal	Protein	Carbohydrate	Cholesterol	Sodium	Fiber	Carbohydrate	Meat	Fat
								Exchanges		
10	<1 g	6 %	<1 g	1 g	0 mg	45 mg	0 g			

MUSTARD

(can be made without wheat, gluten, dairy, eggs, yeast, or refined sugar - see page 9 about ingredients)

Keep this flavorful condiment in your refrigerator.

3 tablespoons tapioca flour
2/3 cup water
1/4 cup dry mustard (Colman's is best)
1/3 cup cider vinegar or Ener-G yeast-free/gluten-free vinegar (reconstituted)
2 tablespoons honey

1/2 teaspoon salt
2 tablespoons fresh grated horseradish (or to taste)
1/4 teaspoon ground turmeric (for color)
dash paprika

Mix the tapioca flour in 1/4 cup of the water until paste forms. Set aside. In small saucepan over low-medium heat, mix together the dry mustard, vinegar, honey, salt, and remainder of water. Gradually whisk in the tapioca flour paste until well blended. Bring to boil, stirring constantly, until mixture thickens.

Remove from heat and stir in horseradish, turmeric, and paprika. Refrigerate in airtight container. Makes 1 cup.

Preparation = 15 minutes. Serves 16 (1 tablespoon each).

Per tablespoon:

Calories	Fat	% Fat Cal	Protein	Carbohydrate	Cholesterol	Sodium	Fiber	Exchanges Carbohydrate	Meat	Fat
25	<1 g	1%	<1 g	6 g	0 mg	71 mg	<1 g	1/2		

TOMATO SAUCE

(can be made without wheat, gluten, corn or refined sugar - see page 6 for ingredients)

If you can't eat commercial canned tomato sauce (it contains corn syrup), make your own with this easy recipe. You may omit the sugar or "jazz" it up with additional herbs and spices.

2 tablespoons chopped onion
1 small garlic clove
1 14.5 ounce can of whole peeled tomatoes or 4 large peeled fresh tomatoes

1/4 teaspoon salt
1/2 teaspoon sugar or honey (optional)
1/8 teaspoon freshly ground black peppe

Puree all ingredients in blender until very, very smooth. Place in small saucepan and cook over low-medium heat for 20-25 minutes or until desired consistency. Makes 1 cup, which is equivalent to the 8 ounce can of commercial canned tomato sauce.

Preparation = 30 minutes. Serves 16 (1 tablespoon each).

Per tablespoon:

Calories	Fat	% Fat Cal	Protein	Carbohydrate	Cholesterol	Sodium	Fiber	Exchanges Carbohydrate	Meat	Fat
10	< 1 g	8%	1 g	4 g	0 mg	200 mg	1 g	1/4		

WORCESTERSHIRE SAUCE

(can be made without wheat, gluten, dairy, eggs, yeast, or refined sugar - see page 9 about ingredients)

This important condiment will be the color of white Worcestershire sauce, but packed with flavor.

1 1/2 teaspoons canola, safflower, or other oil
1 medium onion, chopped
2 large garlic cloves, chopped
1 jalapeno pepper, seeded, chopped
2 cups cider vinegar or Ener-G yeast-free/gluten-free vinegar (reconstituted)
1 cup honey

1 cup water
2 tablespoons fresh lemon juice
2 tablespoons fresh grated horseradish
1 tablespoon anchovy paste (optional)
1 teaspoon salt
3/4 teaspoon black pepper
1/8 teaspoon ground cloves

In large, heavy saucepan over medium-high heat, sauté onion and garlic in oil for about 3 minutes. Add remaining ingredients. Bring to boil. Reduce heat to medium low, simmering until mixture is reduced to 3 cups. Stir occasionally. Mixture darkens as it simmers.

Strain into an air-tight glass container and store in the refrigerator. Makes 3 cups.

Preparation = 1 hour. Serves 96 (1 tablespoon each).

Per tablespoon:

Calories	Fat	% Fat Cal	Protein	Carbohydrate	Cholesterol	Sodium	Fiber	Exchanges Carbohydrate	Meat	Fat
15	<1 g	5 %	<1 g	3 g	0 mg	29 mg	<1 g	1/4		

APPENDICES

BAKING WITH ALTERNATIVE SWEETENERS

This section presents information for those who prefer to use sweeteners other than white sugar. Some basic guidelines are presented below, but each individual recipe may require a little experimentation to achieve the desired results—especially the preferred sweetness.

SWEETENER	AMOUNT TO USE	WHEN TO USE/TIPS
Honey From bees. Color and taste depend on flower source. 20% to 60% sweeter than white sugar.	Use 2/3 to 3/4 cup for 1 cup white sugar. Reduce liquid 1/4 cup. Add 1/4 teaspoon baking soda per cup of honey to neutralize acids. Reduce oven 25°.	All baked goods. Some vegans avoid. Don't give honey to children under age 2, because of possible botulism.
Granulated Fruit Sweetener From grape juice concentrate and rice syrup **(Fruit Source™)**. Light brown granules taste like brown sugar. Not as sweet as white sugar.	Use 1 1/4 cups for 1 cup white sugar. Reduce salt 30-50%. Use plenty of cooking spray on pans or use parchment paper. Don't overmix batter. Keep oven temperature at 350° or lower and adjust baking time.	Cookies, cakes, and puddings. Works better when dissolved in warmed liquid before adding to recipe. Company sources verify that the rice syrup is gluten-free.
Mixed Fruit Juice Concentrate (liquid) Usually made of peach, pear, grape, and pineapple juices plus rice syrup. **(Fruit Source™)**. Fruity-tasting liquid. Light brown color. Refrigerate after opening.	Use 2/3 cup for 1 cup white sugar. Reduce liquid 1/3 cup per cup of sweetener. Add 1/4 teaspoon baking soda per cup fruit sweetener. Reduce oven temperature 25° and adjust baking time. More user-friendly than the granulated version of Fruit-Source™.	All baked goods and desserts, except white cakes and chocolate dishes. If using in fruit pies, drain canned fruit thoroughly since too much liquid produces soggy pie crust. Company sources verify that the rice syrup is gluten-free.

NOTE: Ask your health professional if these alternative sweeteners are safe for your diet.

BAKING WITH ALTERNATIVE SWEETENERS

(continued)

SWEETENER	AMOUNT TO USE	WHEN TO USE/TIPS
Frozen Fruit Juice Concentrate (e.g., Apple, White Grape, Orange, Pineapple) Look for *pure* concentrate, but avoid if on a yeast-free diet.	Same as for mixed fruit juice concentrate—but this is a thinner liquid, so use about 25% less. Add 1/4 teaspoon baking soda per recipe.	Homemade applesauce, cakes, cookies, bars
Fruit Puree Use baby food fruits or puree fruits in blender.	Prune, apple, apricot, banana, pear. Best if used as sub-stitute for 1/2 (not all) of sugar (or fat) in recipe.	Baked goods, e.g., banana in banana bread, prunes in "dark" colored foods, pears in light-colored foods, etc.
Dried Cane Juice (Sucanat® - *Sugar Cane Natural*) Made of sugar cane with water removed. Coarse, amber granulates. Mild molasses taste.	Use same amount as white sugar. Add 1/4 teaspoon baking soda per cup of dried cane juice. Sift before using. Store in dry, cool place.	Cookies, cakes, pies, and puddings, but not white cakes. May be a bit grainy in baked goods unless dissolved in warmed liquid ingredient first.
Date Sugar Ground, dehydrated dates. Coarse, brown granules. Very sweet.	Use 2/3 as much as white sugar. Works well when used in combination with other sweeteners. Store in dry, cool place.	Dissolve in hot water or other liquid before adding to recipe. Works well as top-ping for fruit desserts. May burn in recipes that bake for a long time.
Brown Rice Syrup Made from brown rice and enzymes from barley. Half as sweet as white sugar. Refrigerate after opening. (Lundberg's new version is gluten-free, but others may not be—read the label.)	Use 1 1/3 cups for 1 cup white sugar. Reduce liquid 1/4 cup per cup rice syrup. Add 1/4 teaspoon baking soda per cup of syrup.	Cookies, pies, puddings. Use with other sweeteners in cakes. Makes baked goods crisp. **Caution:** Celiacs must avoid brown rice syrup, unless its gluten-free status is verified.

NOTE: Ask your health professional if these alternative sweeteners are safe for your diet.

BAKING WITH ALTERNATIVE SWEETENERS

(continued)

SWEETENER	AMOUNT TO USE	WHEN TO USE/TIPS
Maple Syrup (pure) From maple tree sap. Dark (Formerly Grade C) best for flavor in baking. Dark brown in color.	Use 2/3 to 3/4 cup maple syrup for 1 cup white sugar. Reduce liquid in recipe by 3 tablespoons. Add 1/4 teaspoon baking soda per cup maple syrup. Refrigerate after opening.	All baked goods, especially cakes. Use only organic to avoid formaldehyde and other possible additives.
Maple Sugar From maple syrup that has been boiled down to granular sugar. Light brown granules.	Use 1 cup maple sugar for 1 cup white sugar. Add 1/8 teaspoon baking soda for each cup maple sugar.	Dissolve in warmed liquid from recipe before using in batters, if possible.
Molasses (unsulphured) Made from concentrated sugar cane juice. Strong flavor.	Use 1/2 cup molasses for 1 cup white sugar. May combine with other sweeteners to minimize strong flavor. Reduce liquid by 1/4 cup.	All baked goods, especially when strong spices are used as in spiced cakes, muffins, cookies, etc.
Stevia Sweet-leafed herb from Paraguay. In leaf, tincture, or powder form.	30-40 times sweeter than sugar. Slight licorice aftertaste.	Recipes require total modification to successfully use stevia. Best used in recipes requiring little sugar.

Sweeteners for Diabetics: You may use your favorite sweetener in these recipes, but make sure the sweetener is designed for baking if you use it in baked goods. You may need to experiment a bit to achieve the desired results. NutraSweet will not work in baking.

NOTE: Ask your health professional if these alternative sweeteners are safe for your diet.

See next page for additional, more refined alternative sweeteners.

BAKING WITH ALTERNATIVE SWEETENERS

(continued)

The following sweeteners are believed to be more highly refined than those on the previous pages. Nonetheless, they work quite well in baking. Here are some guidelines to assure successful results.

SWEETENER	AMOUNT TO USE	WHEN TO USE/TIPS
Brown Sugar Actually white sugar with molasses added for heartier flavor and color. May use light or dark version.	Use 1 cup brown sugar in place of 1 cup white sugar.	When heartier flavor and darker color in baked goods is desired.
Corn Syrup Produced by action of enzymes on cornstarch. Used in many commercial products.	Use 1 cup corn syrup in place of 1 cup white sugar. Reduce liquid by 1/4 to 1/3 cup.	Use in any baked item that can use honey. **NOTE:** High fructose corn syrup <u>may</u> contain gluten from a brewer's yeast extract used in processing.
Fructose Granular version usually refined from corn syrup, although sometimes from fruit sources. A bit sweeter than white sugar.	Use 1 cup of fructose in place of 1 cup white sugar.	Use in cakes, cookies, bars, breads, muffins, or any baked item where honey is also appropriate.
Liquid version also derived from corn.	Use 1 cup liquid fructose in place of 1 cup white sugar. Reduce liquid by 1/4 to 1/3 cup.	Use liquid fructose in same way as corn syrup.
Turbinado Actually just raw sugar with the impurities removed.	Use 1 cup turbinado in place of 1 cup white sugar.	Use in any recipe, but works better in darker colored baked goods.

NOTE: Ask your health professional if these alternative sweeteners are safe for your diet.

BAKING WITH DAIRY SUBSTITUTES

Milk is one of the easiest ingredients to make substitutions for in baking, although some milk substitutes lend a subtle flavor to baked goods and may affect the degree of browning while baking. In addition, read labels to avoid problem ingredients such as casein. Celiacs should avoid versions with brown rice syrup (which may be processed with barley malt).

In place of 1 cup of cow's milk, use:

SUBSTITUTE	AMOUNT TO USE	WHEN TO USE/TIPS
Rice Milk (rice beverage) Be sure to buy brands that are vitamin-fortified.	1 cup. Mild flavor, white color. Looks like skim milk from cows.	In any recipe, although it is slightly sweet-tasting. Make sure it is gluten-free.
Soy Milk (soy beverage) Be sure to buy brands that are vitamin-fortified.	1 cup. Slight soy flavor, light tan in color. Can buy in liquid or powder form (which must be mixed with water.) Powdered version makes lighter color milk.	Best in recipes with stronger flavors so soy taste is masked, if desired, and in baked goods with darker colors since soy milk darkens with heat. Make sure soy milk is gluten-free.
Nut Milk (usually almond) Persons with allergies to nuts should use caution. Ener-G NutQuik is made of almond meal and guar gum.	1 cup. Mild, slightly nutty flavor. Light brown color.	Best in dessert recipes. Tastes slightly "off" in savory dishes.
Goat Milk Available in powdered and liquid form; also in low-fat liquid by Meyenberg. Not recommended for those with true milk allergies, but milk-intolerant can try it.	1 cup. Most closely resembles cow's milk in color (pure white.)	In any recipe. Works especially well in ice cream, puddings and other milk-based dishes. Aseptic and powdered varieties have stronger flavor.
Oat Milk	Not recommended for those with gluten-intolerance.	
Coconut Milk	Very high in fat. Not tested in these recipes. However, many people use coconut milk successfully.	

NOTE: Ask your health professional if these alternatives are safe for your diet.

BAKING WITH DAIRY SUBSTITUTES

(continued)

If the recipe calls for Dry Milk Powder: Use same amount of non-dairy milk powder, but read labels to make sure there are no problem ingredients such as casein. You may also use 3/4 as much goat's milk powder, if approved for your diet. Milk-allergic people should avoid goat's milk, but milk-intolerant people say they can use goat's milk. Or omit dry milk powder altogether and add same amount of rice flour or sweet rice flour. Baked goods won't brown as much without dry milk powder (which is not the same as Carnation instant dry milk). In yeast breads, rising and browning will be diminished without milk powder.

In place of 1 cup evaporated skim milk, use:

SUBSTITUTE	AMOUNT TO USE	WHEN TO USE/TIPS
Ener-G NutQuik or SoyQuik or other non-dairy milk powders. Mix at double strength.	1 cup	Recipes using evaporated skim milk. Flavors will be stronger. Calories and nutrient values will be doubled.

In place of 1 cup buttermilk, use:

SUBSTITUTE	AMOUNT TO USE	WHEN TO USE/TIPS
Use 1 tablespoon fresh lemon juice or cider vinegar or reconstituted Ener-G yeast-free/gluten-free vinegar and enough rice, soy, or nut milk to equal 1 cup.	1 cup (Some non-dairy milks produce a thinner buttermilk. If so, use 2 tablespoons less of non-dairy buttermilk per cup specified in recipe.)	Any recipe calling for buttermilk

Density of Milk: Whether you're using liquid non-dairy milks or mix your own from powder, remember that the thinner the milk the less you'll need. For example, reduce the liquid by 1 tablespoon per cup if you use skim milk in place of whole milk. You may need to experiment a bit to achieve the desired results since liquid milk densities vary by brand and the ratio of powder to water will affect the density of milks made from non-dairy powders.

Lactose-Reduced Milk: You may use lactose-reduced milk in these recipes. However, make sure you can tolerate these milks before cooking with them and be certain to read the label to make sure they contain no other offending ingredients. Also, some recipes may not produce the same results as those with "regular" cow's milk or non-dairy milks.

NOTE: Ask your health professional if these alternatives are safe for your diet.

BAKING WITH DAIRY SUBSTITUTES

(continued)

In place of 1 cup yogurt, use:

SUBSTITUTE	AMOUNT TO USE	WHEN TO USE/TIPS
Goat Yogurt (Persons with true milk allergy should avoid all goat products.)	1 cup	Any recipe calling for yogurt. However, the tapioca in goat yogurt may make baked item "doughy".
Soy Yogurt	1 cup	Not well-suited to heat, but works well in dips, ice creams, and other non-baked items. Won't drain.
Non-Dairy Milk Liquid	2/3 cup	Any recipe calling for yogurt. Best to add liquid in 1/3 cup increments, so you avoid adding too much.

The suggestions offered in this section on dairy substitutes are primarily for baking. Bear in mind, however, that the same amount of milk substitute such as rice, soy, or nut milk can be used in non-baked items—like milkshakes, puddings, ice cream, or smoothies.

Cheese: Although there are several "non-dairy" cheeses such as Parmesan cheese made from rice, soy, or nuts, it is difficult to find one that doesn't have additional problem ingredients. For example, they may contain milk proteins called calcum caseinate, sodium caseinate, or casein. Others include oats (which is off-limits for celiacs) or texturized vegetable protein (which can have various sources, but is often soy.) Also, plain milk may contain one set of ingredients but flavored versions may contain different ingredients.

Sour Cream and Cream Cheese: Soyco makes a rice-based version, however, check the label to make sure it's right for your diet—the milk protein, casein, is present in both items. Soymage makes a casein-free sour cream alternative.

Keep in touch with your natural food store. New, non-dairy cheeses are being developed.

NOTE: Ask your health professional if these alternatives are safe for your diet.

BAKING WITH EGG SUBSTITUTES

Eggs are one of the hardest ingredients to make substitutions for because they play such critical roles in baking. They can be used as binding agents (hold ingredients together), moisturizers (add moisture), or as leavening agents (make things rise) in baking. Generally speaking, egg-free baked goods rise less and have a denser texture than those made with eggs. Here are some general guidelines when modifying recipes to exclude eggs.

Eggs As Binders:
If the recipe has only one egg but contains a fair amount of baking powder or baking soda, then the egg is the binder.

In place of 1 egg as a binder, use:

SUBSTITUTE	AMOUNT TO USE	WHEN TO USE/TIPS
Tofu (soft silken) by Mori-Nu®	Use 1/4 cup for each egg and blend with recipe liquid in food processor until completely smooth before adding to recipe.	Cakes, cookies, breads—although light-colored baked goods won't brown as deeply. Makes very moist baked goods with a somewhat heavier texture.
Pureed fruits/vegetables Apples (or apple butter), apricots, prunes, or pears. Or, pureed vegetables such as corn, carrots or mashed potatoes. Baby foods work well, especially Gerber's 1st which has no additional fillers.	Use 3 tablespoons to replace each egg. Increase liquid in recipe by 1 tablespoon.	Especially useful in baked goods where the flavor of the fruit or vegetable puree complements or doesn't detract from the flavor of the dish (e.g., pureed prunes work fine in chocolate cakes but not in yellow cakes).

You may use liquid egg substitutes in place of real eggs. But please note that liquid egg substitutes actually contain eggs. The yolks have been removed to reduce the fat and cholesterol. *People with egg allergies cannot safely consume these products because they still contain eggs. Also, some egg substitutes contain other problem ingredients such as modified food starch which may or may not be wheat-based.* Read the label.

NOTE: Ask your health professional if these alternatives are safe for your diet.

BAKING WITH EGG SUBSTITUTES

(continued)

In place of 1 egg as a binder, use: (continued)

SUBSTITUTE	AMOUNT TO USE	WHEN TO USE/TIPS
Unflavored Gelatin Powder May use animal derived or vegetable-based (kosher) gelatin powder.	Mix 1 envelope of unflavored gelatin with 1 cup boiling water. Substitute 3 tablespoons of this liquid gelatin for each egg in your recipe. Refrigerate; then microwave to liquefy before use.	Baked goods such as cookies, cakes, breads
Arrowroot, Soy, Lecithin	Whisk together 1/4 cup warm water, 2 tablespoons arrowroot, 1 tablespoon soy flour, and 1/4 teaspoon lecithin liquid or granules.	All baked goods, but preferably those with stronger flavors since the soy and lecithin may affect the overall taste of dish.
Flaxseed	Pulverize 1 teaspoon whole flax seeds in coffee grinder or blender. Combine with 1/3 cup water and bring to boil. Reduce heat and simmer for 3-5 minutes until mixture is consistency of egg whites.	Cool mixture before adding to baked goods. Best used in "dark" dishes since the brown color of flax may discolor baked goods. Mild flavor. **NOTE:** Some celiacs report discomfort due to a slight laxative effect.

NOTE: Ask your health professional if these alternatives are safe for your diet.

BAKING WITH EGG SUBSTITUTES

(continued)

Eggs as Leavening Agents:
If there are no other ingredients that make the baked item rise, then the egg is the leavening agent.

In place of 1 egg as a leavener, use:

SUBSTITUTE	AMOUNT TO USE	WHEN TO USE/TIPS
Egg Replacer by Ener-G (a powder made from potato starch, tapioca flour, calcium lactate, calcium carbonate, citric acid and a vegetable-derived gum) It may not be corn-free, however.	1 1/2 teaspoons Egg Replacer powder mixed in 2 tablespoons water. For double effect, double the amount of Egg Replacer powder in same amount of water.	All baked goods. Flavorless, so won't affect taste of recipe. For added lightness, whip in food processor or blender for 30 seconds.
Buttermilk-Soda See page 156 for making dairy-free buttermilk.	Replace liquid in recipe with equivalent amount of buttermilk (or thinned yogurt if you're not dairy-sensitive.) Replace baking powder with same amount of baking soda, not exceeding 1 teaspoon per cup of flour.	All baked goods, but this technique works best in dishes that don't require a lot of "rising" to look good. such as cookies, bars and flatbreads.

Other Hints When Omitting Eggs (when used as leavening agents)

1. Add air to lighten the recipe by creaming the fat and sweetener together with your electric mixer. Then add dry ingredients

2. Whip the liquid ingredients in a food processor or blender for 30 seconds as another way of incorporating air into the recipe.

3. Add an extra 1/2 teaspoon baking powder per egg. Do not exceed 1 teaspoon baking powder per cup of flour or a bitter taste will develop. As an alternative to commercial baking powder (which contains corn), try the homemade version on page 141.

4. Recipes with acidic liquids such as buttermilk, molasses, lemon juice, or vinegar tend to rise better than those with non-acidic liquids such as water or milk.

NOTE: Ask your health professional if these alternatives are safe for your diet.

BAKING WITH EGG SUBSTITUTES

(continued)

Eggs as Moisture:

The egg's purpose is to add moisture if there are leavening agents in the recipe, but not much water or other liquid in the recipe. For example, the Zucchini Bread on page 38 in this book has 2 eggs, but no additional liquid—although the grated zucchini does add some moisture. The recipe for Zucchini Bread on page 39 eliminates eggs, but adds liquid in the form of honey, milk, and molasses.

Generally speaking, baked goods without eggs are somewhat heavier and more dense than those with eggs. For that reason, slightly increase the leavening agent in your egg-free recipes to compensate for the egg's natural leavening effect. In addition, using liquid sweeteners such as honey or molasses for part of the sugar in a recipe helps compensate for the loss of the "binding" effect of eggs.

In place of 1 egg, use:

SUBSTITUTE	AMOUNT TO USE	WHEN TO USE/TIPS
Fruit juice, milk, or water	2 tablespoons. Increase leavening by 25-50%. May need to bake items slightly longer.	Baked goods such as cakes, cookies, bars
Pureed fruit such as bananas, applesauce, apricots, pears, prunes. (The natural pectin in fruits, especially prunes, traps air which helps "lighten" baked goods.)	1/4 cup. Increase leavening agent by 25-50%. May need to bake items slightly longer.	Baked goods where the fruit's flavor complements the overall dish such as applesauce in spice cakes, bananas in banana bread, apricots and pears in mild-flavored items, and prunes in dark, heavily-flavored items such as chocolate or spice cakes.

NOTE: Ask your health professional if these alternatives are safe for your diet.

BAKING WITH WHEAT-FREE FLOURS

This table presents a summary of the baking characteristics, color, flavor, and storage recommendations for wheat-free flours (and grains) used in this book. General comments are also offered.

FLOUR	CHARACTERISTICS
Arrowroot	
Baking	Good in baking because it adds no flavor of its own and lightens baked goods. If used as breading, produces golden brown crust. Twice the thickening power of wheat flour.
Color/Flavor	Snow white in color. Looks like cornstarch. Flavorless.
General Comments	Silky, fine powder from West Indies root. Used to replace cornstarch or tapioca flour.
Storage	Air-tight containers in cool, dry, dark place.
Bean Flour	
Baking	Two kinds of bean flour: 1) pure garbanzo or chickpea flour, and 2) flour made from a combination of garbanzo and broad (fava) beans (available from Authentic Foods – See Mail Order Sources). Both flours provide protein that is beneficial in baking. Use in combination with other flours to totally (or partially) replace rice flour.
Color/Flavor	Light tan or yellowish. Slight "beany" flavor, especially if flour is pure chickpeas or garbanzo beans—less so if using garbanzo/fava bean combination. The latter imparts a slightly sweeter taste to baked goods, especially pizza crust.
General Comments	Adds important protein to otherwise "starchy" gluten-free flour blends. Not widely available in stores, but can be ordered by mail. See Mail Order Sources.
Storage	Air-tight containers in cool, dry, dark place.
Cornmeal	
Baking	Excellent in corn bread, muffins, and waffles—especially when blended with corn flour. Blue cornmeal can be used in muffins and waffles.
Color/Flavor	White or yellow. Tastes like corn. Blue cornmeal is grayish-blue and has a somewhat stronger flavor.
General Comments	Coarser than corn flour. Often used in Mexican dishes. Used in Polenta. Make sure cornmeal does not contain wheat. Not the same as masa harina which may contain wheat.
Storage	Air-tight container in cool, dry, dark place.

NOTE: Ask your health professional if these alternatives are safe for your diet.

BAKING WITH WHEAT-FREE FLOURS

(continued)

FLOUR	CHARACTERISTICS
Cornstarch	
Baking	Helps lighten baked goods, but use only in combination with other flours—not alone. Most commonly used as thickener in sauces and gravies.
Color/Flavor	Snow white in color. Flavorless, although more noticeable than arrowroot.
General Comments	Highly refined and contributes little nutritional value.
Storage	Air-tight container in cool, dry, dark place.
Potato Starch	
Baking	Excellent baking properties, especially when combined with eggs. Lumps easily, so stir before measuring.
Color/Flavor	Very white. Bland flavor.
General Comments	Very fine, powdery texture. Made from starch in potatoes. Not the same as potato flour, which is made from dried, ground potatoes with skins. Potato flour is heavy and used very little in wheat-free cooking.
Storage	Air-tight container in cool, dry, dark place.
Rice—White	
Baking	A bit dry and gritty by itself, but works fine when combined with other flours. Should be about 2/3 of total flour. The coarser the grind, the more liquid needed.
Color/Flavor	White color. Bland, pleasant-tasting flavor.
General Comments	Milled from broken hulls of rice kernel. Among least "allergenic" of all flours. Mostly starch. Nutritionally inferior since bran and germ layers have been removed in milling.
Storage	Air-tight container in cool, dry, dark place.
Rice—Brown	
Baking	Dry and gritty, but excellent in baked goods. Produces off-white color in baked goods.
Color/Flavor	Off-white color. Mild flavor. Makes baked goods slightly darker than white flour.
General Comments	Higher in nutrient value than white rice since brown rice still contains bran.
Storage	Air-tight container in cool, dry, dark place. Somewhat shorter shelf life due to higher oil content in bran. May want to refrigerate or freeze.

NOTE: Ask your health professional if these alternatives are safe for your diet.

FLOUR	CHARACTERISTICS
Soy	
Baking	Excellent. Works well in baked goods with nuts, fruits, or chocolate. Adds moisture to baked goods. Best when combined with other flours such as rice.
Color/Flavor	Yellow in color. Bland, somewhat nutty flavor—leans toward "beany". Can be camouflaged by mixing with spices, fruit, nuts, or chocolate.
General Comments	Makes crispy coating for breading. Higher in protein and fat than other flours. Short shelf life, so purchase in small amounts to avoid spoilage. A common allergen, so use soy cautiously.
Storage	Air-tight container in cool, dry, dark place. Best if refrigerated.
Sweet Rice	
Baking	Not the same as white rice flour. Manufacturers suggest using in muffins, breads, and cakes although some sources recommend using only small amounts. Helps bind baked goods because of its sticky nature.
Color/Flavor	White, bland in flavor. Easily confused with white rice flour because they look alike.
General Comments	Sometimes called sticky rice or glutinous rice—but doesn't contain wheat gluten. Often used in Chinese cooking. Contains more starch than rice flours, making it an excellent thickener. Helps inhibit separation of sauces when they're chilled or frozen.
Storage	Air-tight container in cool, dark, dry place.
Tapioca	
Baking	Excellent in baked products when it makes up 25-50% of total flour. Lightens baked goods and imparts "chewiness" to breads. Browns quickly and produces crispy coating in breading.
Color/Flavor	Snow-white, velvety powder. "Anonymous" flavor.
General Comments	Sometimes called cassava or cassava starch. Similar to arrowroot and can be used interchangeably.
Storage	Air-tight container in cool, dark, dry place.

NOTE: Ask your health professional if these alternatives are safe for your diet.

WHEAT FLOUR EQUIVALENTS

Use the information in this table to convert your own recipes to wheat and gluten-free—or to modify recipes in this book. Remember, flours have unique characteristics which affect the texture, taste, and appearance of your baked goods.

Use the following amount of flour in place of **1 cup of wheat flour**.

KIND OF FLOUR	AMOUNT
Corn Flour	1 cup
Cornmeal	3/4 cup
Cornstarch	3/4 cup
Garbanzo (Chickpea) Flour	3/4 cup
Garbanzo (Chickpea) and Fava (Broad) Bean Flour from Authentic Foods	7/8 cup (in recipes using 1 cup or less flour, use a 1:1 ratio)
Nuts (ground fine)	1/2 cup
Potato Starch Flour	3/4 cup
Rice Flour (Brown or White)	7/8 cup
Soy Flour	1/2 cup + 1/2 cup potato starch flour
Sweet Rice Flour	7/8 cup
Tapioca Flour	1 cup

Flours from reputable sources will usually measure consistently time after time, although differences in flour milling processes may affect consistency and texture. As you become more experienced with these flours, you will be able to judge if the dough is too dry, too moist, or just right.

NOTE: Ask your health professional if these alternatives are safe for your diet.

SUBSTITUTES FOR WHEAT AS A THICKENER

In place of **1 tablespoon of wheat flour**, use the following:

INGREDIENT/ AMOUNT	CHARACTERISTICS	SUGGESTED USES
Agar (Kanten) – 1 1/2 teaspoons	Follow package directions. Colorless and flavorless. Sets at room temperature. Gels acidic liquids. Thin sauces need less.	Puddings, pie fillings, gelatin desserts, ice cream, glazes, cheese. Holds moisture and improves texture in pastry products.
Arrowroot – 1 1/2 teaspoons	Mix with cold liquid before using. Thickens at a lower temperature than wheat flour or cornstarch, so it's better for eggs or sauces that shouldn't be boiled. Add during last 5 minutes of cooking. Serve immediately after thickening. Clear, shiny. Semi-soft when cool.	Any food requiring clear, shiny sauce, but good for egg or starch dishes where high heat is undesirable. Gives appearance of oil even if none used.
Bean Flour – 3 teaspoons	Produces yellowish, rich-looking sauce.	Soups, stews, gravies
Cornstarch – 1 1/2 teaspoons	Mix with cold liquid before using. Stir just until boiling. Makes transparent, shiny sauce. Slight starchy flavor. Thicker and rigid when cool.	Puddings, pie fillings, fruit sauces, soups. Gives appearance of oil if none used.
Gelatin Powder – 1 1/2 teaspoons	Dissolve in cold water, then heat until liquid is clear before using. Won't gel acid liquids such as fresh pineapple.	Jello puddings, aspics, cheesecakes

NOTE: Ask your health professional if these alternatives are safe for your diet.

SUBSTITUTES FOR WHEAT AS A THICKENER

(continued)

In place of **1 tablespoon of wheat flour**, use the following:

INGREDIENT / AMOUNT	CHARACTERISTICS	SUGGESTED USES
Guar Gum – 1 1/2 teaspoons	Mix with liquid before using. **Caution to celiacs**: has high fiber content and may act as laxative.	Especially good for rice flour recipes
Kudzu (kuzu) Powder – 3/4 teaspoon	Dissolve in cold water before using. Odorless, tasteless. Produces transparent, smooth sauces with soft consistency.	Puddings, pie fillings, and other dishes that must have "gelatin-like" consistency
Sweet Rice Flour – 1 tablespoon	Excellent thickening agent. Sometimes called "glutinous" rice, but contains no gluten.	Sauces such as vegetable sauces
Rice Flour (brown or white) – 1 tablespoon	Mix with cold liquid before using. Somewhat grainy texture. Consistency the same hot or cold.	Soups, stews, or gravies or hearty, robust sauces
Tapioca Flour – 1 1/2 tablespoons	Mix with cold or hot liquid before using. Add during last 5 minutes of cooking. Produces transparent, shiny sauce. Thick, soft gel when cool.	Soups, stews, gravies, potato dishes
Quick-Cooking Tapioca (pre-cooked) – 2 teaspoons	Mix with fruit, let stand 15 minutes before baking.	Fruit pies, cobblers, and tapioca pudding
Xanthan Gum – 1 teaspoon	Mix with dry ingredients first, then add to recipe.	Puddings, salad dressings, and gravies

NOTE: Ask your health professional if these alternatives are safe for your diet.

COOKING OILS

Use this chart to determine which oil is best for you. It's best to consult with your health professional about this decision. The lower the smoking point, the more quickly the oil will burn.

Oil	% Saturated	% Poly-unsaturated	% Mono-unsaturated	Smoking Point
Canola oil	6	32	62	400°
Safflower oil (refined)	10	77	13	450°
Sunflower oil	11	69	20	450°
Corn oil (unrefined)	13	62	25	320°
Olive oil	14	9	77	350°
Soy oil	15	61	24	450°

Source: ***Compositions of Foods***, United States Department of Agriculture.

THE SUBSTITUTE PANTRY

Here is a basic set of ingredients to have on hand when cooking for the special diets addressed in this cookbook.

INGREDIENT	PURPOSE/TIPS
Unbuffered Vitamin C	Acid helps leavening. Instead of cider vinegar, use 1/4 teaspoon per cup to add acid to liquids such as milk.
Baby Foods – Applesauce, Apricot, Prunes, Pears, etc.	Partial replacement for fats and oils. Provides moisture and binds ingredients together in egg-free cakes, cookies, breads, etc. (You may use your own applesauce or apple butter or pureed fruits instead of baby food.)
Baking Powder (cereal free)	Leavens baked goods. Commercial versions often contain corn. See Index for corn-free Baking Powder.
Baking Soda	Leavens baked goods.
Cooking spray (gluten-free)	Use in place of oil to sauté. Prevents baked goods from sticking to pan.
Cream of Tartar	Neutralizes baking soda. Combine with baking soda to make baking powder. (2 parts cream of tartar; 1 part baking soda)
Dry Milk Powder or Non-Dairy Milk Powder	Protein boosts yeast activity in breads and other baked goods. This is not Carnation Instant Milk.

NOTE: Ask your health professional if these alternatives are safe for your diet.

THE SUBSTITUTE PANTRY

(continued)

INGREDIENT	PURPOSE
Ener-G Egg Replacer	Replaces eggs and leavens and stabilizes baked goods.
Extracts (gluten-free) such as vanilla, almond, lemon or butter	Boosts flavor in desserts, baked goods.
Flours (wheat-free) white rice, brown rice, potato starch, tapioca, cornstarch, arrowroot, bean, bean/fava, soy	A combination of these flours can be used as a substitute for wheat flour. See Wheat-Free Flours for flour characteristics and uses.
Gelatin powder (unflavored.) Available in animal or vegetable-based (kosher) form	Binds ingredients together in some baked goods and desserts. Adds moisture to baked goods. (May use agar, instead.)

Gum
  – xanthan
  – guar
	Substitutes for gluten and acts as a stabilizer, emulsifier and suspension agent so dough rises well. Also thickens. Use in baked goods. (Guar gum not advised for celiacs.)

Italian Herb Seasoning	Use this, and your favorite dried herbs and spices to boost flavors in baked goods, salad dressings, and sauces.
Lecithin (granules or liquid) Made from soy.	Softens the loaf and improves texture of bread. Granular and liquid versions measure the same. (Make sure it is pure lecithin and that you know the source is pure soy.)

NOTE: Ask your health professional if these alternatives are safe for your diet.

THE SUBSTITUTE PANTRY

(continued)

INGREDIENT	PURPOSE
Milk (rice, soy, or nut beverage)	Keep liquid versions on hand in aseptic containers (which must be refrigerated after opening).
Sweeteners	In place of refined sugar, use maple sugar or maple syrup, date sugar, honey, dried cane juice, molasses, fructose liquid and fructose powder, or fruit juice concentrates.
Tofu (soft silken) by Mori-Nu®	Helps bind ingredients together in place of eggs. Use firmer (firm and extra-firm) varieties in frostings and cream pies.
Yeast (gluten-free)	Leavening for bread, baked goods. (Red Star, both quick-rising and regular, has no gluten or cereal. Also, SAF from the Gluten-Free Pantry is gluten-free.)
Yogurt	Provides additional moisture in baked goods. Thickens and "creams" sauces. Used to make Yogurt Cheese. May use goat yogurt or soy yogurt (if your diet permits) depending on recipe.
Vinegar (gluten-free)	Use cider, wine, or rice vinegar. If yeast is a concern, use ENER-G yeast-free/gluten-free vinegar. (Distilled vinegar may be grain-based.) Strengthens yeast dough to rise better.

NOTE: Ask your health professional if these alternatives are safe for your diet.

HIDDEN SOURCES OF WHEAT AND GLUTEN

Wheat flour is present in many products, but it isn't always listed as such. Avoid products containing ingredients such as all-purpose flour, unbleached flour, bread flour, cake flour, whole-wheat flour, semolina, or durum because these are alternate terms for wheat flour and will contain gluten. And, yes—white bread contains wheat (and therefore gluten). Also, you must check to see whether your food is prepared in the same receptacle or manufacturing line as wheat-containing foods or somehow contaminated with wheat flour—even though it's not listed as an ingredient. Finally, this list may change over time so you must continually be careful and read labels.

• **Beverages:** Avoid beer and ale, gin, whisky (bourbon, scotch and rye), vodka (if it's grain-based; potato and grape-based vodka are wheat-free), Postum, and Ovaltine.

• **Breads:** Unless the label says "wheat-free", avoid any biscuits, breads, crackers, croutons, crumbs, doughnuts, tortillas, or wafers. (You should also avoid breads made of oats, spelt, kamut, barley and rye because they are similar to wheat and contain gluten.)

• **Candy:** Wheat may be an ingredient (for example, licorice contains wheat flour) or used in the shaping or handling of the candy.

• **Caramel Color or Flavoring:** This may contain malt syrup or wheat starch.

• **Cereal:** Avoid those made from wheat, rye, oats, barley, spelt, and kamut or if they contain malt flavoring or malt syrup. The Celiac Sprue Association/USA also advises Celiac Sprue patients to avoid quinoa and amaranth.

• **Coffee:** Some decaffeinated, flavored, and instant coffees may cause distress for persons who avoid wheat and gluten.

• **Condiments and Baking Ingredients:** Check labels, especially on mixed spices, ketchup, some prepared mustards, mayonnaise, salad dressings, and most soy sauces. Look for wheat-free or gluten-free versions of these ingredients.

• **Dairy Products:** Some flavored yogurts contain modified food starch (which could be wheat). Look for those with pectin (this is fruit). Malted milk, processed cheese spreads, and chocolate milk may contain wheat. Low-fat sour cream may contain wheat.

• **Desserts and Other Sweets:** You'll bake your own pies, cakes, and cookies—but also avoid commercial pudding mixes, marshmallow creme, cake decorations, and marzipan because they may contain wheat flour as a thickener or binder.

HIDDEN SOURCES OF WHEAT AND GLUTEN

(continued)

• **Distilled Vinegar:** Vinegar made from wine, rice, or cider are safe for wheat-sensitive persons. Avoid those made from grain since wheat is often used as a base.

• **Hydrolyzed Plant Protein (HPP):** Can be made from wheat starch.

• **Hydrolyzed Vegetable Protein (HVP):** Labels should list the source of protein.

• **Flavorings and Extracts:** Grain alcohol is often an ingredient. Look for gluten-free flavorings and extracts.

• **Meat, Fish, and Eggs**: Avoid any meat that's been breaded or in which fillers might be used such as sausage, luncheon meats, or hot-dogs. Avoid self-basting turkeys. Buy tuna in spring water rather than oil. Egg-substitutes are not pure eggs but often contain many other additional ingredients—possibly wheat flour.

• **Modified Food Starch:** This could be corn or wheat or some other unidentified food starch. Unless the label specifically states the source, it's best to avoid altogether.

• **Pastas:** You can eat some Oriental rice noodles, bean threads, and commercial pasta made from rice, corn, tapioca, or potato starch flour. Be sure to read labels since some pastas are made from a mixture of flours which may also include flour made from wheat or a member of the wheat family.

• **Soups and Chowders:** Many canned soups, soup mixes, and bouillon cubes or granules contain hydrolyzed vegetable protein (HVP) which may contain wheat.

• **Texturized Vegetable Protein (TVP):** This protein can be made from wheat starch.

• **Vegetables:** Avoid vegetables that are breaded, creamed, or scalloped because this usually involves wheat flour or bread crumbs made from wheat flour. When you see "vegetable starch" or "vegetable protein" on a label, this could mean protein from corn, peanuts, rice, soy—or wheat.

An excellent resource to help you know which commercial products are gluten-free is the Celiac Sprue Association's Cooperative Gluten-Free Commercial Products Listing. See Associations & Resources in the Appendix.

HIDDEN SOURCES OF DAIRY PRODUCTS

Milk and milk products can be hidden in a variety of foods. Your food choices should be guided by whether you are lactose-intolerant or allergic to milk proteins. And, when reading the ingredient list, remember that there are other words used to indicate milk. For example, casein is a milk protein and whey, another protein, is the liquid derived from drained yogurt. Other terms to avoid include: acidolphilus, caseinate, calcium caseinate, hydrolyzed milk protein or vegetable protein, lactalbumin, lactate, lactoglobulin, lactose, and potassium caseinate. Below is a partial list of hidden dairy in commercial goods.

Baked Goods and Cooking Ingredients
Bread
Biscuits
Cakes
Caramel Coloring or Flavoring
Chocolate
Cookies
Doughnuts
Hot Cakes
Malted Milk
Mixes for Cakes, Cookies, Doughnuts,
        Muffins, Pancakes, etc.
Ovaltine (and other cocoa drinks)
Pie Crust (made with milk products)
Soda Crackers
Zwieback

Casseroles and Side Dishes
Creamed Vegetables
Hash
Mashed Potatoes
Scalloped Dishes
Dishes in Au Gratin Style
Fritters
Rarebits

Dairy

Buttermilk	Ghee (clarified butter)
Cheese	Milk (all forms)
Condensed Milk	Non-Dairy Creamer
Cream	Skim Milk Powder
Cream Cheese	Sour Cream
Evaporated Milk	Yogurt
Ice Cream	Whey

Desserts
Bavarian Cream
Candies
Custard
Ice Cream
Sherbets
Sorbet (some versions)
Spumoni
Pudding

Egg Dishes
Omelets
Scrambled Eggs
Soufflés

Meats and Fish
Canned Tuna
Deli Turkey
Hamburgers
Meats Fried in Butter
Sausages

Sauces and Salad Dressings
Butter Sauces
Cream Sauces
Gravies
Hard Sauces
Mayonnaise (some brands)
Salad Dressings (especially boiled)

Soups
Bisques
Chowders

HIDDEN SOURCES OF EGGS

Many commercially prepared foods—or ingredients you buy to prepare your own dishes—contain eggs. Here is a partial list of those items. Be sure to read labels and remember that the ingredient list may not specifically mention the word eggs, but instead use words such as albumin, livetin, ovaglubin egg albumin, ovamucin, ovumucoid, ovovitellin, lysozyme, or egg whites, egg yolks, egg solids, or egg powder.

Baked Goods and Baking Ingredients
Baking Powder
Batters for Deep-Frying
Breads
Breaded Foods
Cakes
Cake Flour
Cinnamon Rolls
Cookies
Donuts
French Toast
Fritters
Frostings
Icings
Malted Cocoa Drinks
Marshmallows
Muffins
Pancake Flour
Pancakes
Pancake Mixes
Pretzels
Waffles
Waffle Mixes

Condiments and Sauces
Hollandaise Sauce
Salad Dressings (especially boiled ones
Sauces (may be thickened with eggs)
Tartar Sauce

Desserts
Bavarian Cream
Ice Cream
Ices
Macaroons
Meringues
Pies (Cream pie filling and some pie crusts)
Puddings
Sherbets
Soufflés

Meats, Meat-Related Dishes
Bouillon
Hamburger Mix
Meat Loaf
Meat Balls
Meat Jellies
Meat Molds
Pate (also called Fois Gras)
Patties
Sausages
Soups (e.g., consommés)
Spaghetti & Meatballs

Beverages
Eggnog
Malted Cocoa Drinks (e.g. Ovaltine)
Wines (may be "cleared" with egg whites)

Other
Pasta (and dishes containing pasta)
Tartar Sauce

HIDDEN SOURCES OF CORN

Corn appears in many unsuspecting places as an emulsifier, sweetener or main ingredient.

Baked Goods and Baking Ingredients

Baking Mixes for Biscuits, Doughnuts,
    Pancakes and Pies
Baking Powder
Batters and Deep-Frying Mixtures
Bleached Wheat Flour
Breads and Pastries
Cakes
Cookies
Cereals
Corn Syrup
Cream Pies
Glucose Products
Graham Crackers
Oleo
Powdered Sugar
Tortillas
Vanilla
Vinegar (distilled)

Beverages

Ales
Beer
Bourbon and Whisky
Carbonated Beverages
Instant Coffee
Milk (in paper cartons)
Fruit Juices
Grape Juice (look for pure grape juice)
Soy Milk
Tea (instant)
Wines (some contain corn)

Non-Food Items

Adhesives and Glue
Bath Powder
Envelopes
Stamps
Talcum Powder
Toothpaste

Condiments, Sauces and Snacks

Catsup
Cheese
Commercial Syrups (e.g., Karo)
Fritos
Peanut Butter
Popcorn
Salad Dressings (e.g., French)
Soups (cream-style)
Tortilla Chips

Desserts

Candy
Frosting
Gelatins or Jello
Ice Cream
Jams and jellies
Puddings or Custards
Sauces for Cakes or Sundaes
Sherberts

Meats, Meat-Type Dishes & Side Dishes

Bacon
Bologna
Canned Peas
Chili
Chop Suey
Gravies
Grits
Hams
Sandwich Spread
Sauces for Meats
Sausage
Vegetables (in cream sauces)

Pharmaceuticals and Drugs

Aspirin and other tablets
Cough Syrup
Vitamin C Preparations

HIDDEN SOURCES OF SOY

Soy appears in a variety of commercially prepared foods, as well as many ingredients.

Baked Goods and Baking Ingredients
Breads
Cakes
Cereals
Cooking Spray
Crackers
Lecithin (derived from soy)
Oils
Oleo or Margarine
Pastries
Rolls
Shortening

Beverages
Coffee Substitutes
Lemonade Mix
Soy Milk

Condiments, Sauces, Snacks, and Soups
Butter Substitutes
Cheese
Soy Sauce (and other Oriental sauces)
Worcestershire Sauce
Salad Dressings
Soup

Desserts
Caramel
Candies
Candy Bars
Custards
Ice Cream
Nut Candies

Meats and Meat-Related Dishes
Luncheon Meats
Sausage (certain kinds)

Miscellaneous
Baby Foods
Bean Sprouts
Pasta from Soy Flour
Tempura
Tofu

HIDDEN SOURCES OF YEAST

Many foods contain yeast, either naturally (such as mushrooms) or because of the way they are prepared (such as fermented products). Below is a partial list of hidden yeast in commercial foods.

Breads, Flours and Mixes
Breads
Cookies
Crackers
Pies and Pastries
Pretzels
Cakes and Cake Mixes
Hamburger Buns
Hotdog Buns
Flours (enriched with vitamins from yeast)
Rolls (e.g., cinnamon, dinner, and other
    yeast rolls)

Beverages
Alcoholic Beverages (e.g., wine, rum, etc.)
Black Tea
Citrus Fruit Juices (frozen or canned)
Fruit Juice Concentrates (frozen)
Ginger Ale
Milk (fortified with vitamins from yeast)
Root Beer
Malted Milk Drinks

Cereals
Barley Cereal (or those with malt)
Oatmeal (certain brands)

Condiments
Barbecue Sauce
Chili Peppers
Horseradish
Ketchup
Mayonnaise
Meat Sauce
Mustard (prepared)
Olives

Condiments (continued)
Pickles
Sauerkraut
Salad Dressings (e.g., French)
Soy Sauce
Vinegars (Ener-G makes a yeast-free pow-
    der that can be reconstituted with water)

Dairy Products
Buttermilk
Cheese
Cottage Cheese
Milk (fortified with vitamins)
Sour Cream
Yogurt

Fruit
Dried Fruit

Meats
Breaded Meats
Canned Mincemeat (not really meat)
Processed Meats, Cold Cuts, Sausage

Vegetables
Mushrooms and Truffles
Tomato Sauce

Vitamins and Nutrient Supplements
Antibiotics (made from mold cultures)
B Complex
Multi-Vitamins with B Complex
Selenium
Vitamin Products (look for yeast-free
    versions)

ASSOCIATIONS & RESOURCES

The following is a partial list of resources for people who must live or choose to live on special diets. Ask your physician about local support groups for people with food allergies, celiac disease, diabetes, or other conditions where certain ingredients must be omitted from one's diet. This partial list is offered as a resource and is not intended as an endorsement of any particular organization or institution.

Allergy & Asthma Network, Mothers of Asthmatics, Inc. 3554 Chain Ridge Road, Suite 200 Fairfax, VA 22030-2709 (800) 878-4403 (help line) (703) 385-4403	American Academy of Allergy, Asthma & Immunology 611 E. Wells Street Milwaukee, WI 53202 (800) 822-2762 (help line) (414) 272-6071
American Diabetes Association, Inc. 1660 Duke Street Alexandria, VA 22314 (800) DIABETES or (800) 232-3472 www.diabetes.org	American Dietetic Association 216 West Jackson Boulevard, Suite 800 Chicago, IL 60607 (312) 899-0040
Asthma & Allergy Foundation of America 1125 15th Street, N.W., Suite 502 Washington, D.C. 20005 (800) 7ASTHMA (help line) (202) 466-7643 aafasupgr@aol.com (support group information)	Celiac Disease Foundation 13251 Ventura Blvd., Suite 3 Studio City, CA 91604-1838 (818) 990-2354; (818) 990-2379 - FAX http://www.celiac.org/cdf
Celiac Sprue Association/USA PO Box 31700 Omaha, NE 68131-0700 (402) 558-0600; (402) 558-1347 - FAX celiacusa@aol.com	Food Allergy Network (FAN) 4744 Holly Avenue Fairfax, VA 22030-5647 (800) 929-4040 or (703) 691-3179 http://www.foodallergy.org fan@worldweb.net
Gluten Intolerance Group of North America PO 23053 Seattle, WA 98102-0353 (206) 325-6980	National Jewish Center for Immunology & Respiratory Medicine 1400 Jackson Street Denver, CO 80206 (800) 222-5864 (Lung Line) (303) 388-4461

MAIL ORDER SOURCES
For Wheat-Free/Gluten-Free Ingredients & Products

If you don't have a natural food or specialty food store nearby, the following companies take phone or mail orders. Contact them for a catalog.

A & A Amazing Foods, Inc. (also called Absersold Foods) PO Box 3927 Citrus Heights, CA 95611 (800) 275-1437 (gluten-free milk powder and liquid)	Authentic Foods 1850 W. 169th Street, Suite B Gardena, CA 90247 (800) 806-4737; (310) 366-7612 (310) 366- 6938 FAX http://pages.prodigy.com/AUTFOODS (garbanzo/fava bean flour, mixes)
Bickford Flavors 19007 St. Clair Avenue Cleveland, OH 44117-1001 (800) 283-8322 (flavorings, extracts)	Bob's Red Mill Natural Foods 5209 S.E. International Way Milwaukie, OR 97222 (800) 553-2258 (503) 653-1339 - FAX www.Bobsredmill.com (flours, grains)
Cybros, Inc. PO Box 851 Waukasha, WI 53187-0851 (800) 876-2253 (flours, breads, cookies)	Dietary Specialties, Inc. PO Box 227 Rochester, NY 14601 (800) 544-0099 (716) 232-6168 - FAX www.colorwheel.com/DS (pasta, flours, cookies, mixes, crackers, ingredients, condiments)
Ener-G Foods, Inc. P.O. Box 84487 Seattle, WA 98124-5787 (800) 331-5222 (206) 764-3398 - FAX www.ener-g.com (flours, ingredients, mixes)	Gluten-Free Cookie Jar PO Box 52 Trevose, PA 19053 (215) 355-9403 (breads, cakes, muffins, mixes)

This list is offered as a convenience and is not intended as an endorsement of any particular company. It was updated when this book was published. However, the names, addresses, phone (or fax) numbers, and e-mail addresses of these companies may have changed as well as the product lines they carry.

MAIL ORDER SOURCES
For Wheat-Free/Gluten-Free Ingredients & Products
(continued)

Gluten-Free Pantry PO Box 881 Glastonbury, CT 06033 (203) 633-3826 (860) 633-6853 FAX http://www.glutenfree.com pantry@glutenfree.com (mixes, ingredients, appliances)	King Arthur Flour PO Box 876 Norwich, VT 05055 (800) 827-6836 (800) 343-3002 - FAX (flours, mixes, xanthan gum)
Miss Roben's PO Box 1434 Frederick, MD 21702 (800) 891-0083 (301) 898-42489 (301) 631-5954 FAX http://www.jagunet.com/~msrobensmissro ben@aol.com (baking mixes, ingredients)	Mr. Spice Healthy Foods 850 Aquidneck Avenue Newport, RI 02842 (401) 848-7700 (401) 848-7701 - FAX (gluten-free, salt-free, fat-free sauces)
Pamela's Products, Inc. 364 Littlefield Avenue South San Francisco, CA 94080 (415) 952-4546 (415) 742-6643 - FAX (mixes, cookies, biscotti)	The Really Great Food Co. PO Box 319 Malverne, NY 11565 (800) 593-5377 (516) 887-0418 - FAX (mixes and flours)

Three Internet news groups provide discussions on important topics:

Celiac Disease & Wheat Sensitivities	Dairy Sensitivities	Yeast Conditions
To join, in the body of an e-mail to: listserv@MAELSTROM.stjohns.edu send the following: SUB CELIAC firstname lastname	To join, in the body of an e-mail to: listserv@MAELSTROM.stjohns.edu send the following: SUB NO-MILK firstname lastname	To join, in the body of an e-mail to: LISTSERV@PSUHMC.HMC.PSU.EDU send the following: SUB YEAST-L firstname lastname

FOOD EXCHANGES

The food exchanges in this cookbook were calculated using nutrient values from MasterCook 3.0, which in turn are derived from the United States Department of Agriculture. Using these nutrient values, calculations of food exchanges are based on "Exchange Lists for Meal Planning", published jointly in 1995 by the American Diabetes Association and the American Dietetic Association.

Following these guidelines, exchanges are given for the major groups: Carbohydrate, Meat, and Fat. Since these recipes are primarily for baked goods, the Carbohydrates are almost always primarily starch. Exchanges are calculated to the nearest 1/4 in order to provide a high degree of precision; exchanges smaller than 1/4 are not reported. If your diet does not require this much precision, simply round the exchanges to the desired precision. Additional nutrient values are offered for each recipe (calories, fat, protein, carbohydrates, sodium, cholesterol, and fiber) so you can calculate your own exchanges, if you prefer.

The following chart shows the amount of nutrients in one serving from each list.

Groups/Lists	Carbohydrate (grams)	Protein (grams)	Fat (grams)	Calories
Carbohydrate				
Starch	15	3	1 or less	80
Fruit	15			60
Milk				
Skim	12	8	0-3	90
Low-Fat	12	8	5	120
Whole	12	8	8	150
Other Carbohydrates	15	varies	varies	varies
Vegetables	5	2	—	25
Meat & Meat Substitute				
Very Lean (VL)	—	7	0-1	35
Lean (L)	—	7	3	35
Medium-Fat (MF)	—	7	5	75
High-Fat (HF)	—	7	8	100
Fat	—	—	5	45

The nutrient values and corresponding food exchanges for each recipe are as accurate as possible, but will naturally vary due to preparation techniques, serving sizes, and various other factors. For best results, consult your physician, dietitian, or other health professional for guidance in using this information.

APPLIANCES AND UTENSILS

People often ask me what type of appliances I use when developing recipes for my cookbooks. I use a Welbilt 2200T bread machine (there are more recent models with more features available), a very simple version that bakes perfect bread every time. When mixing extremely heavy bread doughs by hand, I use an Oster Kitchen Center (which has a heavy-duty mixer). And, I use regular beaters—not dough hooks—for mixing bread dough.

For cake, cookie batters and cooking class demonstrations, I use a hand-held Hamilton Beach mixer. It has a fairly powerful motor, which is essential for some of the heavier doughs. A Hamilton food processor (using knife blade) is indispensable for blending batters and doughs because it is very fast and does a better job of distributing the moisture throughout the ingredients than an electric mixer. In fact, I wouldn't be without this indispensable appliance (which costs about $40 on sale at discount stores.) There are, however, much more expensive versions available.

I bake almost exclusively in nonstick pans because gluten-free batters tend to stick. The darker finish on nonstick pans also helps the browning process. Insulated baking pans (except for cookies) tend to make baked goods somewhat soggy. Be sure to use utensils specially designed for nonstick pans so you don't scratch the specially treated surfaces.

Generally speaking, using several smaller pans in place of one large pan assures that the finished product will rise and bake thoroughly. However, for your convenience I usually offer directions for using both large and small pan sizes.

Serrated knives or electric knives are especially helpful in cutting breads. You can find electric knives in discount stores for around $15. They are also great for cutting pie crusts.

My oven and range are electric Jenn-Aire, but remember that different brands and types may produce slightly different outcomes. Follow the directions exactly the first time you make any recipe, then make changes as needed—such as longer or shorter baking times.

I use waxed paper or parchment paper for baked goods that must be removed from the pan whole, rather than sliced. The new teflon liners, available at kitchen stores or by mail-order, are also great for baking.

INDEX

ABOUT THE AUTHOR

A former university professor and marketing executive with a Fortune 500 corporation, Dr. Fenster graduated from the University of Nebraska with a degree in home economics and was a home economics specialist with the Cooperative Extension Service at North Dakota State University. Her graduate degree in sociology helps her understand the symbolic role that food plays in our lives and how special diets can affect that symbolism.

After discovering her own food sensitivities several years ago, Dr. Fenster studied extensively to find flavorful alternatives for problem ingredients. She understands the importance of a healthy diet and the desire for fine dining—which is all the more challenging when one has to avoid certain ingredients.

She serves as vice-president of her local asthma and allergy support group (affiliated with the Asthma and Allergy Foundation of America) and is a member of the Celiac Sprue Association/USA and the Gluten Intolerance Group of North America.

Committed to helping others eat the dishes they want (without the ingredients they can't have), Dr. Fenster makes radio and TV appearances, publishes books and articles in newspapers and magazines, and consults with health professionals and corporations serving those on special diets. She is an on-line advisor for Veggie Life magazine and a frequent guest speaker at associations and organizations across the country.

If you would like Dr. Fenster to speak to your organization, please call or write:

Savory Palate, Inc.
8174 South Holly, Suite 404
Littleton, CO 80122-4004
(303) 741-5408

What People Are Saying . . .

Many people have improved the quality of their lives by using recipes from the Savory Palate, Inc. Here's what they're saying about *Special Diet Solutions.*

- *Living on a limited diet should not limit the possibilities! This book provides great variety and best of all . . . great taste for our wheat-free lifestyle. Thanks to Carol for developing a pizza recipe that is cause for true celebration at our house!*
  – Nancy Carol Sanker, OTR, Fort Collins, CO

- *Your book will appeal to, and help, not just the celiac or wheat-free diabetic community, but many others on special diets . . . your cookbook will never be far from my fingertips and certainly NOT one of those collecting cobwebs in a dusty corner.*
  – Sara Jones (diabetic celiac), Houston, TX

Here's what others are saying about *Wheat-Free Recipes & Menus*, also from the Savory Palate, Inc. . .

- *Finally! A wheat-free cookbook that's upbeat, informative and good.*
  – Maura Zazenski, Littleton, CO

- *Thanks to you I had the most delicious Thanksgiving dinner. I haven't enjoyed a meal like that in 9 years.*
  –Jennifer Roach, Colorado Springs, CO

- *Each time I make the White Bread, I'm thrilled with the texture and taste. It's the best I've ever made.*
  – Cecile Weed, Garden Grove, CA

- *Carol's recipes make it easy to serve others since the results are every bit as good as the wheat recipes.*
  - Lillian Stich, St. Cloud, MN

ORDER FORM

Name_____

Address_____

City/State/Zip_____

Telephone (   ) _____

Please send the following items to the address above:

	QUANTITY	PRICE (Canada & UK add $5)	TAX (Colorado Residents only)	TOTAL
Special Diet Solutions: *Healthy Cooking Without Wheat, Gluten, Dairy, Eggs, Yeast, or Refined Sugar*	_____	$15.95	$.60 per book	_____
Wheat-Free Recipes & Menus 275 recipes for breads, desserts, entrees, sauces, salad dressings, etc. Designed for those who <u>must</u> avoid wheat and gluten … but <u>won't</u> give up anything else!	_____	$19.95	$.75 per book	_____
Bookmarks (handy summaries at your fingertips)				
Baking With Wheat-Free Flours	_____	$1.50	$.20	_____
Baking With Alternative Sweeteners	_____	$1.50	$.20	_____
Baking With Dairy Substitutes	_____	$1.50	$.20	_____
Baking With Egg Substitutes	_____	$1.50	$.20	_____

Shipping & handling ($3 per book) _____
(Canada: $5)

Total Amount Enclosed _____

Please allow 2 weeks for delivery

☐ Check   ☐ Visa, MasterCard, Discover
(payable to Savory Palate, Inc.)

Account Number_____

☐ Money Order

Expiration Date_____

Customer Signature_____

SAVORY PALATE, INC.
8174 South Holly, Suite 404
Littleton, CO 80122-4004

In Colorado
(303) 741-5408

Outside Colorado
(800) 741-5418 (orders only)

FAX (303) 741-0339